Radiance Rising

Ravenwolf

First Paperback Edition: April 2021

ISBN: 978-1-63877-144-9 (print)
ISBN: 978-1-63877-145-6 (e-book)

Hyperbole Publishing
www.houseofravenwolf.com

4

Stories of Hope, Love & Empowerment

Hey, you ... yes, I'm talking to you.
I don't care what you've heard or been told, but you matter.
You're more than enough, and I'm glad you're here.
I know it's hard but try to stop listening to the people who don't know you or don't really care.
They don't know where you've been or the mountains you've had to climb to get to where you are.
I know you think you're a survivor, but I'm here to tell you that you're more than that.
You're the hero of your own story.
It's time to stop trying just to get by and to start growing and loving yourself.
I know all you see sometimes are your scars, failures and mistakes, but they don't define you.
You write your story and your legacy, and it's your time to rise out of the ashes.
I realize you've been down, broken and lost, but you can't start rising until you've hit rock bottom.

The fire that has tried to swallow you whole isn't your end, it's where you will find your strength and forge your courage.

Stop telling yourself what you can't do and start believing in yourself … if you don't, who will?

No, you're not alone and your voice matters.

How do I know?

I've been right where you are, and I know how it feels to be hopeless.

But now you have a choice to make.

You can choose to stay in that dark place, or you can start clawing out of the abyss.

You are enough.

More than that, you're amazing.

You got this, no matter how hard or long it may take ...

Day by day, step by step, start believing in the power of your dreams again ...

Remember those?

The hopes you once had and forgot along the way?

It's time to find those again and take back your voice.

You've been beaten down, pushed away and left for nothing.

You've been asking for a sign …

Well, this is it.

I'm talking to you.

Take my hand and let's start over.

Maybe we don't have all the answers or know where we are going, but we don't have to.

You're not alone.

You're loved and you're special.

Stop listening to the voices and start listening to your soul.

You were meant for more, so take a deep breath and look for the light ...

A little more every day.

It may not be easy, fast or painless.

But together, you and I can do this.

You just have to decide that you're done living in the past and dwelling in the darkness.

I'm here, holding out my hand, asking you to join me.

It's your story, and it's time to start writing a new chapter.

Where shall we begin?

With you.

You've had the answers all along ...

Now it's time to start listening to your own voice.

My Best Qualities

I had always worried that my personality was
too much for some people.
Often, people didn't know how to take me, and
I thought that was my fault ...
My fault for being a little over the top, a little too
outspoken and a whole lot of spunky sass ...
Truth is, it wasn't about me being too much of
anything –
It was about others not being able to handle
my big personality.
Yes, I always have something to say, and I
don't hold back, choose my words carefully or
tiptoe around anyone.
That's just not who I am or will ever be.
I wear my emotions on my sleeve, and I am
real, true and genuine.
With me, what you see is what you get, no
less, no more.
I used to think all of those things were flaws,
but I know differently now.
Turns out, those wonderfully authentic qualities
are my best features.
My people absolutely adore who I am because
they know they can always take me at face

value, and no matter what, I'll always have their back.

Sure, I'm a beautiful mess a lot of days and forget what I'm doing while I'm doing it, but that's just part of my charm.

I'm socially awkward sometimes, and I inadvertently share things that can offend sensitive people –

Not because I'm trying to hurt feelings or make anyone uncomfortable ...

It's just who I am, and I don't plan on changing for anyone.

I'm loud sometimes, I'm awkward other times, but I'm a lot of fun, I'm passionate and I'm totally unforgettable.

You'll never meet another person like me, and that's probably a good thing.

I don't think the world could handle two of me, and that's just the way I like it.

I'll keep on loving my people hard, living my life to the fullest and enjoying each day ...

And every moment.

Maybe I'm nowhere close to perfect, maybe I'm a disaster some days,

But you can always count on me to tell it like it is.

So, if you can get past the silly sarcasm, the bad jokes and snorting laughter, you'll find that I'm one of those people you want to keep around.

You've been gone so long I wonder wistfully if you were ever truly real.

The times we had, the love we shared, the memories we made ...

All seem to dissipate into nothingness as I think back to us and what we had.

The flash of images that run through my mind evoke a mixture of emotions ... happiness from our laughter, sadness from missing you and regret from you not being here anymore.

I think back to being in your arms and the moments I wanted to never end.

We swore to each other that we were meant to be and that our love was forever.

It turns out that sometimes, love alone isn't enough ... time can be a cruel master that takes away even the most precious things ...

But it makes me treasure even more the beautiful love we shared.

The memories make me smile ... and cry.

I miss you so much it hurts, and I wish we had just a little more time together.

I know I'll be able to see you again someday, but right now, I'm an emotional mess as the feelings wash over me.

I fight back the tears when our favorite song plays and flash my bravest smile when someone asks about you.

All I can do is hold onto the joy we once had. It was love, it was real and it was powerful.

I keep those precious droplets of joy in my heart and long for a time when I might hold you in my arms again.

I wouldn't trade any time we shared for the rest of my days – I treasure every moment, every smile and all the memories we created along the way.

You were the first to love me in a way I had never known ... for who I was.

You accepted and adored me for the person I had fought to become.

I don't know what tomorrow will bring, but I do know that I'll see you tonight ... in my dreams. At least there, I'll be forever happy.

Until then, I'll make the best of what I have, hold onto the happiness and keep hoping.

The sun always rises.

Even in my dreams.

I Should Come With My Own Warning Label

I'm not a number on a scale or a cliché, I'm a person.

Just so happens, I'm an awesome, fabulous and amazing person.

If you get caught up in what society thinks is ideal, you'll miss the chance to experience all the things that are truly wonderful about me.

Because they're focusing on all the things that aren't really important.

Forget the unrealistic standards and what the world seems to think is acceptable.

I don't fit into a box or label, and I never will.

I'm a real and genuine person who defies the norm and shines brighter because I own who I am.

You can love me for the amazing person I am, or you can judge me like others do ... That doesn't define me or tell my story ... That's what fake people do to make themselves feel better, so they don't have to take a long look in the mirror.

I don't care if everyone likes me, accepts me or appreciates me, but they will respect me.

I am a beautiful person with a huge heart and an amazing soul.

Try to define me with a size, number or label? Good luck.

I should come with my own warning label.

"Handle with care due to extraordinary awesomeness."

I'm not a number on a scale, a clothing size or a three-letter acronym.

I'm a person, and an amazing one at that.

So, accept me or reject me, I'm still gonna be great.

My life is what I make it,

not what anyone else thinks it should be.

So, if anyone needs a size zero,

Then they can look elsewhere.

I'm real with a lot of love to give, and I'm not changing for anyone or anything.

I'm beautiful because I say so, and that's what matters.

It's my opinion that counts most of all –

if anyone can't love me for me, then that's their loss.

You can't measure heart in a number or see someone's true beauty from the outside.

The real beauty is the depth of their soul and the purity of their heart.
Get to know me and you'll know exactly what I'm talking about.
I own my style and love my looks,
And I don't care what anyone else thinks.
If I don't believe in myself, no one else will either.
I'm a beautiful mess and a perfectly disastrous imperfection at times,
But I'm always true to myself.
That is and always will be good enough for me.

She's not cold or distant, she's anything but what they would have you believe.

No, she doesn't let anyone take advantage of her and she won't let just anyone past her walls … but she has her reasons.

Everything that she is, everything that she has learned, has come from a life of struggle and heartache.

She's made bad decisions and she's chosen the wrong people to love, but it never kept her from holding her head high and still believing in love.

People who don't try to understand her or see past her steely resolve will always misinterpret her facade as hostile or bitter, but they couldn't be more wrong.

She's had to learn how to protect her heart from all the people that she used to let hurt her. She's had to fight for her happiness every step of the way, so she's learned to appreciate the joy in all the moments of life – both big and small.

She's had to claw, battle and dig deep to make it through some of her days ...

But she's still standing.

More than that, she's got a smile on her face and fire in her heart.

Life can't bring her down – it already tried that and failed.

She's been through hell and back, that's how she became the fire that sparks her spirit.

She's not easy to love or quick to know, but she's worth the effort – any effort – because a woman like her doesn't come around often.

Those who seek to love her must have patience, truth and authenticity in their actions or she'll walk away.

She's been lied to, hurt and broken so many times that she's lost count ...

But that's what made her strong; that's what forged her strong will.

She's learned her worth the hard way after being put down, mistreated and taken for granted – she vowed long ago to never let anyone treat her that way again.

People think because of her smile and gentle laugh that she's just like everyone else ... And they're so very wrong.

She's the fire you don't forget and the diamond that sparkles after all the struggles.

She'll never settle, be disrespected or be treated as just another option.

Rain or shine, bad days or good, she's always true to her word and real in her actions.

She doesn't need a partner, charity or pity ...

She knows who she is and what she wants ...

Love – for herself, for her people and for the things that matter.

So, when you meet her, just accept her as she is and love her how you can ...

To know her, love her and be a part of her life is to appreciate someone very special.

After all, the most broken people have the deepest love of all.

Because That Means I'm Done

I told you before that if we ever got to a point
where I stopped caring, I would be done.
Not fighting, crying or being angry ...
No reconciliation, no working through things ...
just done.
Because slowly, with every fight, each night
spent crying and the passing of angry words
between us, a little more of my love for you
died.
I wish I didn't feel this way, but I can't help
what heart tells me is true.
I'm not mad or emotional about us anymore ...
I'm just numb, and that's the worst place to be.
I can't bring back what was there before, and I
can't make my heart feel differently.
I'm just not there anymore.
I'm not in love with you now, not like I was ...
and I won't ever be again.
I'm not doing this to hurt you, I'm giving you the
respect you deserve and being honest with
you.
I will always love you, and you'll always have a
special place in my heart, but when I'm done ...
I'm just done.

There's no coming back from this ...

And I know it hurts you, but I can't live a lie.

We've come too far, and my heart whispers what my head already knew.

I can't manufacture love, and I can't promise you something that is gone ... and those feelings I had aren't there anymore.

We tried to make this love into forever, but we were never meant to be.

Some people come into your life for a season, a reason or a lifetime, and there's so much I've learned from you.

So, I'll never regret us, for I learned ...

What I don't want in a life or love story ...

And most of all, what I'm willing to accept.

I deserve to be a priority, and you never really thought I was important enough for that.

So, while it hurts to look at you with tears streaming down your face, I know it's the right decision: it's time to find our ways on different paths ...

For a time, it was beautiful, it was love and it was us ...

But it was never meant to be forever.

You'll find someone someday who loves you how you want to be loved, but it won't be me.

I'll look back on this time and smile at our memories while continuing forward.
That, for me, will be enough.
So, I'm saying goodbye to us so I can say hello to a new me, a happier me.
Losing someone and moving on is always a little sad, but I know it's for the best –
For both of us.
I hope on day you'll understand why I feel the way I do.
That you'll come to see that what I did I did for both of us ...
Because you deserve to be happy too –
And you never would have found that with me.

Let Go of the Past. Empty Hands Are Easier To Hold

I know you've been hurt before, and I wish I could take that pain away.
I see the distrust in your eyes and the fear in your soul as you're afraid to believe in me or my love.
I can't ask you to trust me, but I can ask you to give me the chance to earn your trust, day by day through love and patience.
I know it's not easy to let your walls down, but I realize you're worth any amount of effort ...
So that's what I will do ...
Love you, respect you and appreciate you in all the ways, both big and small, every day.
All I ask is that you meet me halfway and that we work together to communicate and love unselfishly.
I don't have all the answers and I don't know what tomorrow will bring, but I know that we belong together ...
I've known that from the very first moment our eyes met.
In that instant as our souls connected, I could just feel you, and you felt like home.

I know the hard road you'd traveled, the struggles you'd survived and the love you were fighting to believe in.

I'm here now, and you won't ever have to face the storms alone again.

Let go of the past and the pain that weighs you down.

Open your heart and your hands that were once full of the painful past, and we can start a new chapter for us both.

Take my hand and, together, we can build a beautiful future.

Every day won't be easy or painless, but we can always find the joy in the small moments of our lives.

Heart to heart and soul to soul, we can write a love story for the ages ...

Beautiful and intimate ...

Just the way you've always wanted to love.

Me, you and forever.

I tried so hard to be what you wanted, and it just wasn't enough.

I gave you my heart, and I thought we would be forever, but I was wrong.

I don't know if you just fell out of love with me or never really loved me at all ...

And I may never know the truth.

You told me all the reasons why you we're walking away, and all I could do was cry ...

Partly because I didn't understand but partly because I deserved better.

I did everything, gave you everything, but it wasn't enough ...

Which is one of the hardest feelings to experience – not being enough.

Apparently, I was too much of the things you didn't like and not enough of the things you wanted ...

Which breaks my heart.

I'm going to move on after a lot of tears and probably a few sleepless nights, even though deep down I know this is for the best ...

I just wish I could convince my heart of that.

I would never have been what you wanted, no matter how much I tried to change ... which really isn't love at all.

Unconditional, real love is accepting and appreciating someone just the way they are.

I've learned from you the most valuable lesson of all:

You can't change to make someone love you, because you'll end up not liking the person you've become.

I lost parts of myself trying to be what you said you wanted, and I'm never doing that again.

If someone can't love me for who I am, then they don't deserve me.

I'm done lowering my standards and accepting a love that isn't true.

Maybe I'll end up alone, maybe I'll have to wait a long time, maybe love will find me tomorrow ...

But at least I'll make my journey through life the way that makes me truly happy ...

Being who I am instead of what someone else thinks I should be.

After all, my happiness is what matters most. Love on my terms or not at all, that's my choice from now on.

Because of you, I'm finally free to find myself,
my love and my truths ...
Just the way I've always wanted.

Darling,
Make no mistake about why I love you.
It's not about the things we have, the places
we go or the activities we do together.
It's so much more than that.
It's just you that I need and want, without the
fancy outfits or expensive accessories.
The person that I love beneath all the glitz and
grandeur.
Real love doesn't need expensive gifts or
grandiose jewelry and watches,
Extravagant trips or fancy things – those are all
grand ideas,
But they'll never come close to what matters.
It's simple, really.
You and me, nothing more and nothing less.
Today, tomorrow and forever.
I want to feel you pressed against me,
I yearn to immerse myself in the connection
between your soul and mine ... I crave your
heart beating as one with my own.
Two becomes one in every way that matters.
Forget what the world thinks.

I'll always fight for your love and the things that you value most ...

What I truly need is you needing me.

What happens in the quiet of the night,

When we are snuggled up close,

That's the feeling I can't live without ...

The love that covers me whenever you're by my side – the happiness and joy you bring me is more than mere words can ever describe.

All I really want is to spend the rest of my life, waking up next to you.

If home is where the heart is, then I belong with you.

Because you had my heart ...

From the first moment I saw you.

You have always been and always will be ... my happily ever after.

All my life, I've heard a lot of the same things …
I'm a handful, I'm too much, I'm a lot to take in.
Well, all I can say to that is good –
If I'm too strong for most people's taste, then
I'm doing something right.
I'm not trying to be memorable, stand out or be
different …
I'm just unique.
People that shine brighter catch the eyes of
others because of who they are, not because
they're trying to.
Weaker men would try to tell me to tone it
down, scale it back or be a little less me.
So, I did what anyone should do when I heard
that …
I turned it up even more.
If they can't handle me at my normal level of
amazing, what makes them think they can
handle me at any level?
They can't, they won't, and I don't really care.
I've never sought approval to be who I am nor
asked anyone's permission for my personality.
I just am who I am without apology or regret.

Sure, I may stick my foot in my mouth by saying the wrong things sometimes, and I may not be the quietest one around, but you'll always know where you stand with me and what I think ... however that plays out.

There are a lot of people pretending to be a lot of things to impress a lot of others who really don't matter.

What counts is what I think and the love I have for myself and my people.

I'm always real, authentic and genuine ... and not everyone likes that.

Oh well, that's their loss.

Asking me to tone it down is like asking the sun to stop shining,

So, I think I'll keep doing what I do best and be the best version of me that I can be.

I may not always be pretty, I may not always be put together, but at least I'll always be true to myself.

So, for all those people who told me I'm "too much" or "a lot," you're right.

I love too much, I trust too much, I care too much, and I live too much ... if that's even possible.

No, I'm a lot of all the things that matter – soul depth, down to earth, fun, loving and loyal ... Nothing and no one will ever change that.

I'm not asking for your permission to fly; I'm just going to keep spreading my wings and soaring like I was always meant to do.

Maybe one day you'll stop worrying what I'm too much of and start appreciating me for the amazing person I am.

Until then, I'll keep flying high, loving hard and losing myself in the moments of my life.

You always said you loved me for who I was,
that you wouldn't change a thing.
We both know that wasn't true.
There were little signs along the way that I
chose to ignore, hoping that they didn't really
mean anything.
How wrong I was.
You didn't want me for the person I was, you
wanted me to change into what you thought
you wanted ...
And truthfully, I don't think you had any idea
what that was, maybe you never will.
In fact, you don't need a partner, you want
someone to do for you what you won't do for
yourself.
You would never admit it, but you want
someone to worship you, do whatever you ask
and then love you as well.
I don't want a project; I want a partner.
I'm not going to be your lover, your maid, your
mother and your moneymaker.
That's not fair to anyone, and that's why I'm
walking away now.

I know you'll try to tell me that you'll change,
but that's a broken record I've heard too many
times before.
I've already lost too much of myself trying to
love you, and I'm done sacrificing my dreams
and desires to make you happy ...
Because you won't ever be content.
I don't even know if you truly know what it
means to love someone the right way – in all
the ways that matter,
Not according to what they can do for you.
A relationship is supposed to be a give and
take, but I don't think you got the memo,
Because while you've got the taking part down,
you don't have a clue how to give ... And I'm
done trying to ask for your affection, attention
and love.
I should never have to fight for that.
So, I wish you the best in wherever life takes
you, just know that I won't be waiting for you
anymore at the end of your days hoping you'll
love me the way I deserve.
This will hurt and it will be hard, but even the
thought of leaving feels like a burden has been
lifted – and that's how I know I'm doing the
right thing.

I'll always love you and keep the happy memories in my heart, but I'm choosing now to take back my life and find myself again.
I deserve the kind of love that is unconditionally beautiful and loyally unselfish.
And instead of asking anyone else to do that for me, I'm going to love myself the way I should have all along.
It won't be easy, it won't be fast, but it will all be worth it in the end.
So, I'm taking the first steps on my journey back to who I'm meant to be ...
Freedom never felt so wonderful as it does right now.

She never meant to go down the hard roads
that she did, it's just how her life turned out.
She didn't choose her story ...
Her story chose her.
It's been a tale of heartache and heartbreak,
falls and failures, struggle and loss.
But even more than that, her story is one of
rising from the ashes, getting stronger with
very mistake and becoming more beautiful
after she was broken.
They'll call her distant, cold or unforgiving –
that's just because they don't bother to try to
see past her steely façade ...
Not to keep others out, but to protect herself.
She's been hurt countless times before by
lovers, friends and even family ...
And she has a bitter taste in her mouth from it.
So, maybe she doesn't welcome everyone into
her life with open arms, not because she's
standoffish, but because she's more careful
now who she lets get close to her.
She vowed to never again let the people who
didn't deserve her time or love past her walls ...

anyone who has gotten close to her has earned it.

She's worth that and so much more.

Most people don't understand her, and men always seem to have an opinion about her.

But then, weaker people always put down the strongest souls that they can't tame.

She's not changing to please anyone and she's not pretending to be anything she isn't.

She's real, passionate and always there for the people she loves ...

The rest have to prove they're worth her affection.

Maybe she's not the most popular person, but she'd rather have a few amazing friends than countless fake ones.

So, don't mistake her tough exterior – she has a heart of gold and the deepest of souls.

But she will always keep her head, standards and hopes high, because she's driven to be better and always rise above the struggle of everyday life.

So, when you meet her, take in the beauty of a woman who has been broken in the fire of her life and born again.

She's one of a kind and rightfully so – she's survived what most never could,
And she's done it with a smile on her face and love in her heart.
She'll always be that one lady who can't be defined, contained or easily understood ...
Just the way she likes it.
She is and will always be ...
Unforgettable.

There's just something special about when I wrap my arms around you from behind, a myriad of feelings sweeps over me that words fail to convey.

The warmth of your body pressed to mine, our hearts beating in unison ... well, that's just the start.

Perhaps it's all the things that your embrace tells me without saying a word.

Your arms tell me that you're there for me, through good times and bad, no matter what comes our way.

I just feel safe in those moments when I'm engrossed in you – your touch and scent seemingly make the world melt away as I drift off into all that is you.

You immersed into me, nuzzling me with delicate kisses – as if the promises of your love are woven into each sweet touch.

The feeling of being completely lost in you is an experience unlike any other.

Your arms wrapped tightly about me, your skin pressed to mine, those are the moments that I'll always treasure.

46

It's those times when the serenity of the starry night has breathed its last gasp into the fading day that our love is limitless.
Two souls unified into a singular consciousness that eclipses the realm of the ordinary ... that is us in those moments.
Hugs from behind.
Something so simple that can set your soul on fire,
Make your heart race,
Yet all the while soothing your spirit
And calming your mind.
That's something I want from you ...
For the rest of our lives.

Gorgeous in All My Flaws

I gave up trying to be perfect a long time ago, and it was the best thing I've ever done.
Trying to please all the wrong people for all the wrong reasons was the wrong choice for me.
I'm never going to be flawless, and I'm not going to try to be.
I'm a wonderful mixture of moods, emotions and charisma that is absolutely lovable.
Sure, I don't know where I'm going most of the time, and I don't have a clue about why I'm in the mood I'm in, but that's just part of my attractiveness.
Whether my hair and makeup are a mess – if I even remembered to wear makeup at all – or if I'm completely put together, I'm the same gritty, real and down to earth gal all the time.
I may cry at the drop of the hat or burst into laughter for no reason whatsoever, but I'm always authentic and genuine.
I own my flaws and celebrate my scars, because they tell the story of my journey, my failures and my history ...
And I wouldn't change who I am or where I've been for anything.

There's a unique beauty in my brokenness and a distinct wonder in my gorgeous mess, just ask anyone who knows me.

Whoever really knows me always appreciates me for everything I am … the good, the bad and the silly.

Sure, I don't have it together all the time, but truthfully, I don't have to.

I'm fine flying by the seat of my pants and figuring it out as I go.

Maybe I've gotten lost a time or two, but I always seem to end up where I'm meant to be.

It may not always be pretty, but it's always true … just like me.

I know who I am and what I want, and I own every step of my journey – laughter, tears and all the other stuff in between.

I may not be who I originally set out to be, and I may not be the model of a person that everyone thinks I should be, but I'm an amazing woman who loves hard, lives fully and never gives up on her dreams.

If you ask me, that's a pretty good way to be.

She'd been down some hard roads and there were many times she didn't think she could go on ... but she always found a way.

She was much like anyone else except for one distinct difference: her heart and soul refused to allow her to stop believing in all the things that had broken her ... even the failed love that had shattered her into countless pieces.

Her friends told her that she should step back, that love was a fruitless endeavor, but that's not who she was.

She was a deep soul with a loving heart, and no amount of heartbreak would change who she was or what she wanted.

She knew that real love involved great risk, and she was prepared to keep pushing forward in her search for love.

She was one of those rare creatures who still believed in magic and would love hard whenever there was love to be had ... Unconditionally.

She knew her worth, and while she would never settle, she gave people chances that others wouldn't.

Her journey was one of healing, hope and love.
Love for herself, for her people and for the life
she led ... and also of forgiveness for those
who had hurt her.

It was the essence of who she was, and she
would never let pain or disappointment change
that.

So, as she healed day by day, she loved even
harder.

She would never listen to the negativity or the
whispers that love wasn't real ...

Her heart and soul told her differently.

She didn't have the answers, but she didn't
have to – that's the beauty of life.

Every day is a new chance to uncover joy,
meet new people and open your heart.

They'd call her foolish, discount her hope, but
she was a lover, a dreamer and a believer ...

And nothing would ever change that.

For her, love would always be the answer.

Now and for always.

Give Yourself Permission

You've been thinking about stepping out and taking that chance for a long time.
Yes, I'm talking to you.
You've let all the uncertainties and risk weigh you down, keeping you from doing what you've always wanted.
I'm here to tell you that you may never be ready enough, things will never get less scary, and you may always feel unprepared.
No matter what you've been wanting to do, it's time to stop second guessing yourself and start believing in yourself.
Yes, taking chances can be scary, and that will never change.
But some opportunities only come along once, and you may never get this chance again.
Don't be a person who looks back in a few years and wishes that they had stepped out onto that ledge and made their move.
I won't tell you it will be easy.
I won't tell you it will be painless.
I won't tell you that you'll succeed the first time.
I will tell you that you can do it.

You've waited a long time to make this move and you've had your eye on this for a while ...
What are you waiting for?
Whether it's someone you like, a career change or even opening a business ...
Life's too short to not take the chances you've longed to try, no matter how big or small.
Take the trip. Try the cake. Change career fields. Open the business. Buy the new clothes.
It's time for you to spread your wings and fly.
You may get some bumps and bruises along the way, but you got this.
You're afraid of failing, but that's just part of taking a chance.
You'll fail – we all do ...
But you don't have to stay down.
Keep getting up, keep moving forward and you'll make it work.
So, as you're staring at this crossroads wondering how you can get started, I'm telling you to take a leap of faith.
Step into the unknown and seize this chance.
Close the chapter on what held you back and open the door to new opportunities.
I believe in you.

The time is now, and the story is yours to write ... Pick up the pen and begin a new chapter. You'll be glad you did.

A Strong Woman Won't Beg, She'll Just Walk Away

She's not a woman who will ask or beg for attention and affection; she has too much self-respect to chase a man.

She's been down that road before, and she knows the heartbreak of vying for the love of a man who didn't really want her ... It never turned out well when she tried to force someone's heart to love ... only with her heart in pieces as she wanted something clearly not meant for her.

She realized that affection must happen naturally, and no amount of coaxing, begging or asking will turn anything into real and lasting love.

She learned that lesson the hard way, and she's never forgotten it.

Now, she knew what she deserved, and she would no longer compete for attention, settle for less than she wanted or be okay being just an option.

They'd call her high maintenance, and she'd just smile and reply,

"No, I have high standards."

She stopped trying to force the issue and instead let the suitors chase her.

Love must be natural or it will never be real ... and she was prepared to be alone before she lowered her expectations.

Sooner or later, someone would come into her life and realize her worth ...

And take the time to unravel her mystery.

She was a complicated woman with complex needs, but she knew her value and would hold out for the one who saw past her eyes and touched her soul.

Until then, she'd stay strong, live free and never settle ... Most of all, she'd do it all on her own.

She knew what made her happy and was quite content to keep enjoying her life until someone came along who was good enough to make her want to share it.

That was her choice and her journey ...

She knew she was more than one in a million ... No, she was one of a kind –

And that's the only kind of love story she wanted ... Unforgettable, unbelievable and of course ...

Once in a lifetime, just like her.

She had experienced ordinary love from men
in her past, and she realized a truth about
herself from all those failed love stories: she
needed more.
She yearned for a deeper, more passionate
love that would fill her soul and stoke the
flames of her heart.
No, lackluster love and ordinary feelings would
ever be enough for her.
She needed all of the things that drove her
senses into overdrive … and more.
Day trips to anywhere without a map,
Passionate kisses in the rain,
Long talks in the dark about secrets, feelings
and all the things that made her feel alive.
She'd tried all the regular types of love and
they would never fill her soul.
The things that she dreamt of – that would be
her love story special – she was told those
were just foolish fairy tales and fantasies ...
But she knew better.
She would keep holding out for the love she
deserved, and she refused to settle for less.
She knew it was out there –

Butterflies in the kiss, passion in the touch, depth in the soul connection ...

All the feelings that she longed to experience, with someone that just understood her from the beginning.

They'd call her hard to please or difficult, but that was just because they were okay with average.

She wasn't and didn't care what anyone thought.

She'd rather be burned alive from the passion of white-hot love than to slowly wither away in a numb existence ...

So that's what she wanted and that's what she'd have.

Until destiny came knocking on her door, she'd just keep dreaming, living and thriving with everything she had.

She knew true love was worth waiting a lifetime for ...

She didn't know if her dream would happen tomorrow or next week, but it would happen ...

And when it did, it would be worth all the heartache and tears along the way.

After all, she was the hero of her story ...

So, she kept writing it the way she wanted.

Strong, beautiful and free ...
And destined for an amazing love.

Yeah, I'm someone who you can't help but
laugh at.

It's okay, I laugh at myself, too.

I snort when I laugh, I make weird faces when I
don't realize, and I say hilariously inappropriate
things sometimes.

I'd tell you that I don't mean to be awkward and
strange, but that's totally not true.

I love being the way I am, and I wouldn't
change it for the world.

I'm the friend you can call at the last minute
and invite on a trip to nowhere, and I'll join you
while laughing all the way.

I know I don't fit in, and that's always been my
plan.

I may be ridiculous and weird sometimes, but
I'm never boring.

Yeah, you never know what I'm going to do or
say, but that's part of what makes me colorful
and fun.

Most of all, with me, what you see is what you
get.

I'm always real and authentic – you can take me at my word, and you'll always know where you stand.

It's hard sometimes to stay true to yourself in a world that's in love with fake perfection, but I'm okay standing apart from the crowd.

No matter what happens, you know I'll always have your back and be there to help you pick up the pieces of life's pain.

Sure, sometimes I'm confusing and a little different …

I don't even know what I'm doing half the time myself.

I just do what I do, which is show up, stand up and speak up … with the unique flavor that only I can provide.

I'm a friend who you know will tell you like it is, and you can count on me to keep things interesting, down to earth and lively.

I may be one of a kind, but I'm brave enough to be real, loyal and true to my values and my people.

So, buckle up, buttercup, I'm always down for an adventure ...

Let's go find some fun and lose ourselves in some mischief.

Today is for living, so let's do some of that.
Me and you, the wind in our hair and sun on our faces.
Two weirdos on a journey to fulfill our souls ...
Sounds pretty magical if you ask me.

How You Build a Home

All my life, I have sought peace and happiness
in others, only to be disappointed along the
way.
Broken hearts and promises line the path of my
past, each time stinging a little more than the
last.
I thought I could find the answers in others that
I didn't know how to find in myself ...
Only I wasn't asking the right questions.
Once I stopped looking outside for the truth
and started diving deeper into my soul, that's
when the answers finally made sense.
I had been broken so deeply so many times
that I thought I needed others to help put me
back together again ...
And I couldn't have been more wrong.
Only I knew the journey I had to take and the
fire I had to become.
No one could tell me how to get there or the
choices to make ...
It was always ... me.
I picked myself up and dusted myself off time
and again, a little stronger each time.

I didn't know where I was going or even how I would get there, I just knew I had to keep going.

I had to find my way back home – to my truths, to myself, to my soul.

I had to love myself to feel comfortable in my skin … and I knew that was no easy task,

For the demons that whisper of your flaws and insecurities can be deafening at times …

But I kept going anyway.

I didn't just find the answers to the questions I had asked for so long, I found so much more than that.

I discovered myself, my self love and most of all, I realized where I truly belonged.

I found my home on my way to finding myself, and it was the most unexpected beauty of all.

I was finally where I was meant to be all along, and I found it within.

Home isn't a place or destination, it's a feeling …

And I'm happy as I've ever been being home … where I found the love and peace I had been missing for so long.

At home.

In my heart, in my soul,

Where it had been all along,
Just waiting for me to come back to where I belonged.
In the place where I put myself back together again,
Where I learned to finally love my broken self
... and where I know now that it all starts inside me.
Home.

Take Me With You

I don't care where we go,
Or what we do,
So long as I'm by your side,
With love in our hearts.

We don't know what tomorrow will bring,
For it is never promised,
So, let's live in this moment,
Until our love overflows with emotion.

The world around us can fall apart
And time may cease to be,
But so long as I have your hand in mine,
There's nothing we can't do.

So, let's soak in the beauty of today,
Let's lose ourselves in a cocoon of love,
Cherishing, kissing and relishing each other,
Letting passion completely overwhelm our
senses.

Let's jump off the edge of today
Into an oblivion of love's doing.
No matter how far we go

Or how long it takes.

Or how hard we love ...
We will always have each other,
Heart to heart, deeply in love ...
Forever and always we will truly be.

I've finally started to understand that life seems to be a moving target.
It took a lot of bumps, bruises and falls to realize that every day isn't going to be a win.
I have days when I don't want to get out of bed and just taking a shower seems to be a monumental task.
But there are also days when I hop out of bed, ready to conquer the world, and I feel like I can do anything.
There's no rhyme or reason to why my days are a hodgepodge of ups and downs, but I guess that's just how life works.
I don't have all the answers and, most of the time, I don't even know the questions.
It's a battle to slap a smile on my face at times, while other days I can't stop laughing.
I've learned to take the small victories on the bad days – a stranger's compliment, a delicious cup of coffee or even just a happy phone call with a friend –
That's how I push through the hard times, the days when I can't seem to find the energy or motivation to push harder and rise above.

But I know those are the days that matter most – when I have to dig deep, fight harder and really make the best of the worst.

Anyone can sail through the easy days – we love the times when everything is going right, the world is good, and anything seems possible ...

No, I'm a warrior spirit who finally understands that life isn't about the big victories or the easy days; it's about finding the light on the bad days and pushing your way through to whatever joys you can see through the storms.

So, yeah, it will rain and pour, and storms may threaten to wash away my resolve, but I'm no longer letting those days define me.

I've stopped asking for the rainstorms and challenges to cease.

Now, I'm strapping on my boots, putting on the best smile I can find and tackling my days head on.

I'll still get wet, I'll still slip and fall, but at least now, I'm learning how to dance in the rain.

I sit here in the dark, holding my phone and just wanting so much to send you a text … a message … anything.

You're on my mind and in my thoughts now like you are so often.

But just as soon as I type something out, full of the feelings I want to share with you … I just delete the message and sigh deeply.

I want to tell you so many things – so many emotions I can't tell you that are just stuck in my head, unable to get out.

It's a hard place when you can't share what's in your heart with someone you care about.

I don't know how you'd respond to my words – or if you'd even respond at all.

Frankly, I can't risk hurting my heart again.

I know to care deeply about someone is to put yourself out there, and I'm just not ready to go there yet.

Truthfully, I don't know I'll ever be that ready again.

It's a strange mixture of fear, excitement and curiosity that I can't get past.

Maybe something will happen and one day, I won't delete the message I've typed out to send you … maybe.

Or maybe I'll just keep battling these demons in my head that tell me that I'm not good enough, that I should just stop trying to ask anyone to love me.

Those are the whispers I hear when it gets so quiet at night, borne of a life full of heartbreak and insecurity.

They're so hard to ignore, those little demons that want you to give up and wallow in misery …

Because it's easy to stop believing in yourself when you don't think anyone does.

The light from my phone snaps me out of my spiraling thoughts, and I half-heartedly pick it up.

"Probably nothing," I think wistfully.

Wiping my eyes, my breath stops.

A text from you.

My heart races as I open the message to read it.

Never have two words ever meant more to me than they did in that moment.

"Wanna talk?"

I half laugh, half smile and I nervously debate which of 29 different responses I should send. I type and delete almost a dozen before I just go with my first instinct.

My fingers shake as I type, out of nervous excitement.

"Of course … I'd love to."

As your call pops up on my screen, I smile.

Sometimes, when you're lost in the darkness, you just gotta find something to believe in and try to find the light.

In that moment, I found my path back in the most unexpected way.

Sometimes in the middle of an ordinary day, life gives us little miracles of hope.

This one was mine and I wasn't letting go.

I deserve to be happy, so I'll take it.

I don't believe in luck, accidents or chance. I
didn't find you by sheer possibility, you were
always the one meant for me.
I didn't always know your face or name, as we
were written so long ago in the stars.
From the first moment I saw your face, the very
instant I heard your voice, I just knew.
It's hard to describe how you know until you
do.
There aren't words for how deeply I feel for you
or any way I could ever truly convey how much
you mean to me.
You've changed my life and calmed my soul in
a way that I didn't even know I needed.
So, when people remark about how lucky I am
or the good fortune I had in finding you, I just
smile and nod.
When you finally find the one meant for you,
you realize that chance doesn't exist, because
we belong together, and always will.
The way our souls connect, the manner in
which our hearts collide and the passion we
feel isn't anything other than meant to be ...

And I plan on spending the rest of my life
showing you just how beautiful you are to me.

I know I'm not the easiest person to love
sometimes; I can be an emotional basket case
some days ...
But I don't ever mean to be.
I've always loved you so very deeply, and I
appreciate how you've stood by me through it
all.
I realize that there are going to be those days
when I push your patience to the limit with my
constant upheaval of emotions, frustrations
and wild moods.
Always remember that behind my dizzying
array of tears, loud words and sometimes
crazy ideas is a person who loves you dearly.
We've come so far together – our life and love
has grown so much that I don't have the words
to express my thankfulness for you ...
How you treat me with delicate care sometimes
and how you seem to know just what I need
when I need it ... it brings tears to my eyes.
I'm a challenge, a beautiful mess and some
kind of wonderful chaos, but I'm all yours, and
beneath all of my wacky ways and random

moods is a person who can't imagine life without you.

Those times when life gets me down and I'm coming up for air?

That's when I'm so grateful you're there, holding out your hand.

I know that come what may, we will stand beside each other, heart to heart and soul to soul ...

It won't always be easy, and it won't always be painless ...

But our love will be worth it ...

Always and forever ...

Thank you for always having my back when I need it most.

I don't know how everyone else's love stories go, but because of you, ours will always be my favorite.

She's never asked anyone to feel sorry for her
– she's strong in so many ways the world will
never understand ...
Not because she's wanted to be strong, but
because her life never gave her any other
choice.
Her story is one like that of many others – of
heartache and heartbreak, of loss and failure,
of struggle and disappointment ...
Except that she never accepted defeat.
She picked up the pieces so many times and
just kept going.
She never wondered why her or asked for an
easier journey ...
She just kept climbing because that's just who
she is and the way she has always been.
She'll never ask for a handout or help; she's
learned the hard way to depend on herself and
expect nothing from anyone else.
People would often tell her how they admired
her fortitude and loved her strength – she
would just nod and smile warmly.

They won't ever know the price she's paid to be tough and the fire she has walked through to keep going sometimes.

The same fire that she had to become in order to survive the storms of her life.

She hasn't had a day without struggle or had anything just given to her, for her life has never been easy ...

But that's why she appreciates everything so very deeply ...

That's why she feels the emotions and victories so much – she's endured the darkness for so long, the light is so much brighter each and every time she finds it.

She's not one to do anything halfway – whether it be working hard, playing hard, or just loving with everything she has ...

She's never left anything unsaid, undone or untried.

It's caused her more than one broken heart and countless sleepless nights, but that's how she lives and loves – giving it her all.

And it's exactly that, her journey of hard times and bad days makes her cherish the good times, the good people and the joys of love just that much more than most anyone else ...

The emotions of love and passion are ingrained into her soul so very deeply ... Anyone who sees past her gritty facade and has the patience to take down her guarded walls realizes that she is one of the most amazing creatures that they will ever encounter ...

Whether they are friends or lovers, one peek, one touch, one moment and they know without any doubt that a woman like her is remarkably beautiful ...

For the most broken women have the deepest love ...

And hers is the deepest of all.

I'm taking this chance to love you now, soaking up this moment and immersing myself in your affection.

Tomorrow isn't promised to any of us, so I'm going to seize this day ...

To accept you unconditionally, love you unendingly and cherish you adoringly.

I'm giving you my whole heart and soul, for without great risk, there cannot be great love.

Let's do all the things we've always dreamt of ... appreciating all the small moments of our love that make our hearts smile.

Losing ourselves in the powerful sensations of our love ...

Kissing in the warm afternoon rain,

Cuddling in the crisp morning air,

Holding hands as we watch the sunset fade into oblivion.

I want to know all of you in the ways I know myself ...

Naked and bare, my soul is connected to yours in the most intimate ways I never knew possible.

Your heart in my hands, I will always protect and honor you with fierce devotion and protective loyalty.

Most of all, I want to experience you in all the ways the world will never know ...

The soul filling, passionate loving and deepest truths knowing that meld our heart beats into one.

We were always meant to be, and such shall we always remain.

Two souls that found each other against impossible odds and from miles apart ...

Our spirits connected and our hearts intertwined as love blessed us, at long last.

Tomorrow may never come and the stars may fall from the night sky, but I'll use my last breaths to utter the words of just how very much I love you ...

And I always will.

Our forever will always be my favorite love story.

Loving Them Doesn't Mean You Have To Stay

She sat down and buried her face in her hands, fighting back tears, because she knew what she had to do ...
And it hurt worse than almost anything she could remember.
She loved him and had for so very long, but she had come to realize that sometimes, love alone simply isn't enough.
They had been through so much together, all the ups and downs that life can throw at you ...
So, her heart was heavy and conflicted.
It whispered to hold on ... keep trying,
But she was too far gone.
The joy of their love had long since faded, and she couldn't even remember why they were fighting to stay together ...
It was the fights she remembered all too well.
His mean words and spiteful actions in the heat of the moment had taken a toll on her, and she finally admitted the truth she had resisted for too long:
She wasn't happy anymore, and no amount of communication, effort and date nights could

mend her heart that he had torn apart, piece by piece.

She knew he would never understand and that he would blame her with cold words and even hateful names ... but she was resolute.

She'd always love him, but she was going to find her own way now, without him.

She couldn't fix him, save him or change him – and she shouldn't have to try to ...

She knew it wouldn't be easy, she'd miss him, and it would hurt, but it was more important for her to be happy than to stay in a relationship that was more misery than joy.

It's scary to take the first steps alone when you haven't been by yourself in such a long time ... But there was a sense of relief in her choice to step away.

Her heart, though conflicted, began to feel lighter ... she noticed the feeling of a burden beginning to be lifted ...

And that's when it all changed.

Her soul started to find the happiness again, and her sense of self appreciation began to return.

It would be a long and arduous road, but she was finally ready.

Maybe she'd stumble a time or two and maybe even shed a few tears along the way ...

But she was finally free to love herself and choose what mattered most every day: herself and her happiness.

She'd been through the rain, now it was time for her rainbow ...

And she couldn't help but smile.

She deserved everything, starting with her new self ...

Beautiful, strong and free.

As I look over at your still form, I can't help but smile as I watch you sleep.

In that moment, all I know is that my heart is full.

My whole world is beside me, peacefully lost in slumber, and there's nothing more I could wish for.

We've been inseparable since we met, even if one of us is lost in sleep.

Those are the times when everything just feels right:

The world is quiet, and the night is serene as I softly stroke your hair with the rise and fall of your breaths.

I could stay in this feeling forever as my soul sighs, content and at peace as I feel you against me.

You're all I could have ever asked for and much more … you've changed my world just by being a part of it.

All the things I feel and want to say flash through my mind as I watch you sleep …

I'm just so thankful for you – the life and love we share is special in ways words can't describe.

They say it's the big things that are important, but as I look over at you, I'd tell you the little things are just as noteworthy ...

As I soak in the beauty of this moment, I know that these are the memories and feelings that will fill my heart ...

For the rest of my days ...

And in those days, I will love you always.

An Old Perfume, An Old Song, An Old Memory

I made a wrong turn, and suddenly some familiar sights greeted me that I hadn't seen in ages ...
Including one that I'll never forget.
Our favorite restaurant, where we met and made so many great memories.
I pulled over and felt a mixture of emotions as the past came rushing back – things I hadn't thought about for the longest time.
It's funny how something can trigger such an outpouring of emotion – whether it's a song, a place or even a smell ...
It takes you back to another time when you were a different person.
A smile crept across my lips as I thought of the joy that I experienced in that restaurant, with you.
It's been long enough now that the pain of us doesn't sting or haunt me like it used to, and I'm able to appreciate the beauty of what we had instead of drowning in the ugliness of the end.

I wonder what you're doing now, and I hope you're happy.

I wouldn't change a thing about what happened because I'm happier now than I've ever been.

What I learned about myself when we split up made me stronger and wiser, so I'm in a good place.

It doesn't mean that I don't miss you a little at random times like this, but you're right where you're supposed to be:

In my heart, not my life.

Some would say it's sad that we didn't work out, but I would respond that we were never meant to be.

I learned so much about myself and about love that I'm a better person for having gone through it.

I'll always cherish the happy memories and smile.

For a time, it was beautiful, it was us and it was love.

Remember To Live In Between All the Doing

It took me a long time to realize that I don't have to be everything for everyone.
I've always tried to do too much and stressed myself out as I overloaded my plate with just too much … stuff.
When I finally realized that there wasn't a rush to do it all, that I could take the time for myself and that the doing wasn't worth the stress ...
That's when it all changed.
I got so caught up in trying to help and love the people in my life that I forgot to keep living, and I started losing the joy of the moments that reminded me that I'm truly alive.
I stepped back, inhaled deeply, started to evolve my thinking and just ... slowed down.
Rushing in the doing of all the things never made me feel better, and it didn't change the world … all it did was make me miserable.
Once I finished one thing, three more popped up for me to tackle.
I'm done living that way.

I'm going to be present, soaking in the beauty of the moments, appreciating the little things and just enjoying my life.

Sure, there'll be times when I have to hustle and bustle, but I'm not going to let it consume my energy and stress me out any longer.

I don't want a life of stuff, I want a legacy of love, memories and moments.

I'm going to throw back my head, spread my arms and fly in the glorious wind that blows through my hair.

Maybe I won't get everything done in a day, but life's not a race, it's a journey.

I'm going to chase the things that fill my soul: Connection with amazing friends, warm coffee on a chilly morning, glorious sunsets and the knowledge that I'm living every day to the fullest.

It'll never be perfect or without rain, but neither am I.

I'll never look back and wonder "what if," because I'll lose myself in the adventures that will change my life.

No more rushing, stressing and worrying ... It's time for me to truly live ...

And now is my chance to fall in love with being
alive every day.
These are the moments that will fill my life ...
And I'm going to enjoy them all,
Starting now.

As I Lay Here Wondering, Are You Aching for Me Too?

I look over at the clock, and it's well past midnight … and I can't even begin to sleep. The eerie silence of the house clings to me like a cloak, weighing me down with the heavy air of solitude.

My eyes are drawn to the other side of the bed where you would once lie beside me, peacefully dreaming.

The emptiness drives me to the point of tears as the feelings of missing you wash over me. Since you've gone, nothing is the same.

I expect to hear your voice greeting me as I come home, and yet there's no sound.

I look at my phone as if your name will pop up and … nothing.

I try to dig down and hold onto the happy thoughts, but that gets harder and harder with each passing day.

My life is different now without you in it, and I've struggled to make peace with that.

Some days are harder than others, and I can't help but cry myself to sleep sometimes.

But as more time passes, it seems to get a little easier.

Maybe I'm just more accustomed to being alone or being without you, I don't really know.

I look over at where you used to lie beside me, and my heart still aches for you.

My mind races and wonders if you think of me too – do you long for me as I do for you?

I know I have to start finding my joy and letting you go, but it's so hard.

My friends try to help and encourage me, but I just don't know who I am without you anymore.

I tell my heart every day that what's meant to be will always find a way ...

If you stay gone forever, then we were never written in the stars as I'd always dreamed.

It's hard to lose the one thing you thought would always be there – you, me ... us.

As I roll over and clutch a pillow where I'd once be holding you, I bury my face and cry ...

For us. For you. For what we lost somehow.

I know I'll feel better as the first rays of sunlight brighten my eyes, but right now I let my grief wash over me.

I know I'll look back and realize this was the way it had to be for me to reclaim my strength.

That doesn't make it any easier or hurt any less.

For now, I'll hold onto the happy memories, positive thoughts and know that this, too, shall pass.

I'll find my way back to myself and my happiness, but I know I'll shed more tears before I'm there.

I know the aching for you will slowly go away, but it still hurts, the longing does.

I don't know when or how, but I'll get past this.

Sometimes, you make a few detours on the way to your forever.

I guess you were always meant to be one of mine ... and I'm okay with that.

I'll be fine ... because I always am.

That's just what makes me beautiful –

All this brokenness I'm working my way through ...

I'm strong, I'm a fighter and I always find my way ...

One day at a time ... that's all I can manage right now.

It may not be pretty, it may not be easy,
But at least I'll always do it my way.

Finding Your Worth and Then Finding the Worthy

She had bounced from relationship to relationship, seemingly always ending up in the same place ...
Heartbroken and alone.
She didn't know what she was doing wrong and why she always seemed to end up holding the pieces of her heart.
Her friends would watch her choose all the wrong men for all the wrong reasons and would inevitably be there for her to help her through the breakups ...
Without judgement or opinion, they'd hold her heart as she tried to put herself back to together again.
Amidst the tears and endless sleepless nights, at the end of another broken road of love, something inside of her snapped.
Maybe it was out of frustration, anger or perhaps she just had an awakening ...
She'd tell her friends later that she didn't know what sparked her realization.
Maybe her soul was just weary and tired of her heart being broken ...

But she finally understood that it wasn't what she was doing wrong in love, it was what she wasn't doing for herself that led her here.

For far too long and for all the wrong reasons, she identified herself through her relationships and found her worth there too.

She'd been too busy chasing love and kissing frogs to love herself the way she deserved.

She'd stopped doing the things that made her soul happy and tried to fix partners that she should never have tried to save to begin with.

She made it all about them and never about herself ... and with men who didn't care about her needs to begin with.

They basked in her attention and enjoyed her affection, and for a while she was too busy trying to please them to see how empty and unfulfilling it was for her.

But she had finally hit the wall and was done turning her heart outwards anymore.

She stopped trying to find love and started trying to find herself instead.

She didn't have the answers and didn't know what the future held, but at least she knew what she was worth and would never again settle for less ... Not from herself and definitely not from any man.

Anyone who didn't value and appreciate her worth didn't deserve her either.

Alone and uncovering her strength, she finally found the love she had been missing all along ... Love for herself.

That was when her story changed, and her heart began to heal.

One dream, one hope and one day at a time. She was discovering her truth that had gone overlooked for so long: she was and always would be more than enough.

She was worth so much more than any man had given her credit for, sadly, but now, that was changing, she would make sure of it.

She finally found the answers and love she had sought all her life ...

Within herself.

In Search of Life

For so very long, I sought love, around every corner and in everyone I met. I didn't how and when I'd find the one meant for me to love and hold for always.

Time passed and my heart was torn apart, many times over and deeper each time, I traveled the broken roads, looking for the love that I found so wonderfully in you.

I wasn't waiting for love any longer, as time had moved on and my hopes were dimmed, I had despaired and started thinking, sadly, that maybe, love wasn't meant for me.

Instead, I began to better myself and find the love for whom and what I could become, each and every day chasing and falling in love with myself and being alive in every moment.

So, on that fateful day when our eyes met, and I knew the answer to all the questions I had always asked in search of love ... I realized in an instant you were the one.

The universe has a way of working things out
when you least expect in ways unforeseen.
And I as look at you now, heart in my hands,
I'm reminded ...

Why I'm so thankful it never worked out with
anyone else ... because we were always meant
to be.

Strong Women Feel Pain, They Just Don't Let It Break Them

She isn't strong because that's what she wanted to be ... She didn't choose her story – in fact, it chose her.

She holds herself together with beautiful composure and magnificent courage ...

For as the world thinks she has it all under control, she's almost dying inside.

But that's what separates her from the rest is that you'll never see her break down, lose her cool or fall apart.

The facade she has mastered is evident to everyone she meets – they would never believe she cries herself to sleep.

To all who know her, she's a beacon of glowing hope and strength.

But her extraordinary courage in ordinary situations isn't because she's being heroic ... not in the ways that anyone would think ... it's just who she is.

If people knew the struggles she has overcome, the pain she has endured and the mountains she's climbed, they would be amazed.

The woman who falls apart behind closed doors is the same smiling face that greets the world every morning.

She hurts in ways most will never understand and braves the pain with a resolve that would bring most men to their knees ...

She wasn't given any other choice, so she does what she has to do to keep moving forward with a pep in her step and a light in her heart ...

Pain has almost wrecked her more times than she knows and, still, she carries on.

She feels every broken heart and every harsh word.

The difference between her and the rest?

She doesn't let the pain break her.

She's so many things – warrior, survivor and dreamer ... and so much more.

When all she wants to do is fall apart, she unfurls her wings and flies higher.

That's who she is and always will be:

A strong woman ...

Amazing, resilient and free.

I used to look around and wonder how everyone else seemed to keep it all together when some days, I was on the verge of falling apart.

What was I doing wrong?

I soon realized I wasn't alone – so many of my friends told me that they, too, faced uphill battles a lot of the time.

It's hard to be happy when you feel like you're constantly fighting just to make it through your days sometimes.

That's when someone dear to me shared a sentiment I'll never forget.

"It's okay not to be okay."

I was stunned.

I never thought anyone else struggled like I did because they certainly didn't show it.

I realized that they were just better at building a convincing façade ...

Somehow, the knowledge that I wasn't alone changed everything for me.

To know that my friends, the people I met every day – many of them felt just like I did – was like a breath of fresh air.

I don't want anyone to struggle, but sometimes, it's just a part of life for us all.

We all battle small challenges every day, it's just that some of us have learned how to rise above … stronger and better.

I know now that it's okay not to be okay every day ...

I can cry in the shower when I'm upset, I can scream in the car when I get frustrated, and I can struggle and ask for help without it being the end of the world.

I'll never have all the answers, and I won't know where I'm going a lot of the time, but what matters most is that I keep going.

I'll keep my face to the sun and the darkness of despair can't bury me anymore, no matter how hard it gets.

I'll always have those days when nothing goes right and even my hair doesn't want to cooperate, but I know now I can handle those things – whether they're huge or tiny – and I'll make it through.

It's okay not to be okay, whether it's for a moment, an hour or a day ...

I don't owe anyone an explanation, and I'm going to make it through whatever storm has crashed down on me.

After all, you can't have rainbows without a little rain.

When the rain is coming down hard and you think you can't go on, that's the time you have to do the hardest thing of all ...

You have to put the hardship aside, hold your head up high and just dance in the rain.

I know you've been holding on, lost in the sea of struggle without an anchor for too long.
You've been hoping for a sign, something that will show you the path out of the ashes ...
From the fires that have been trying to burn you to the ground.
Yes, I'm talking to you.
You've been battling for so long that you can't see the light anymore.
Yes, life is hard, and it feels like the weight of the world is on your shoulders.
Yes, you're going to fail, you're going to stumble, you're going to be brought to your knees.
I'm here to tell you that isn't the way your story ends.
You're more than you've been giving yourself credit for and you're stronger than you've ever realized.
How do I know?
Because we are the same, you and me.
I've been down that road that you've been stuck on, and I'm coming back for you ...

I'm holding out my hand and telling you that you're not alone.

More than that, you have greatness coursing in your veins, and it's time to stop surviving now ...

It's time to start living, growing and thriving.

Use that fire that tried to consume your soul and forge a new path out of the darkness.

I know you've been down and out, you've been bruised and broken, but darling, that doesn't define you ...

Where you've been is just part of your story ...

It may be a tale of failure and flight, misery and mistakes, but not anymore.

Stop expecting the next disaster and start believing in yourself.

Take back your power – no matter how long and hard – and start a new chapter.

Turn your setbacks into comebacks and fight for your dreams.

You've lost your magic along the way because you've just been living day to day for as long as you can remember.

No more ... that stops now.

Make up your mind to climb your way out of the mess that has tried to swallow you whole.

Each day, in little ways, begin to rediscover the things that make you feel alive.

Do what you need to do to begin finding your joy again.

It's your time to rise from the ashes as the fire that can't be diminished.

I know you've been hurt, broken and so many have walked away from you.

That's their loss.

If they can't accept you at your worst, they don't deserve you at your best ...

I'm telling you that you can do this.

If you can't find the hope and belief in your heart, take some of mine,

Because I believe in you.

And I know that your dreams, your desires, your goals are just on the other side of believing.

I can't say it will be easy or painless, but I can say it will always be worth it.

This is your time to start dreaming again of all those things you thought you couldn't have ...

Because you deserve all that and more.

So, yes, life is tough ...

But darling, so are you.

You got this.

Laying in your arms, I tried to find the words …
any words to describe this – you – us.
I couldn't.
Your body pressed against mine, bodies
seamless as our hearts pulsed to the same
rhythm ... in that instant, the world was perfect.
The beauty of the moment, the timeless
perfection of your angelic form embraced in my
grasp ... to describe the feelings in that
moment?
Beautifully impossible.
There were no words, in this language or
another, that could begin to describe the
powerful emotions that enveloped our souls,
seemingly suspended in time.
I thought back to the sleepless nights spent
alone, often desolate and bereft of hope ... a
solitary tear escaped down my cheek as I
wondered why ...
Why I saw couples everywhere, yet,
was I not deserving of someone to love, to love
me?
Why were my nights spent cold and alone

while so many others basked by the hearth of love's fire?

Those painful memories melted away as I stroked your soft hair.

My lips pressing against you in a soft, slow kiss that lingered wonderfully.

Finally, love had found me … after a life spent longing.

Your peaceful breathing calmed the restless winds of my soul, the angst that had permeated so many of my loneliest nights.

Indeed, every exhale from your beautiful lips seemed to be the soothing breeze of a warm wind that caressed my spirit.

Suddenly, I was a master of words who could find none, for there are some moments that letters on paper will never do justice … and as my hand slid along your supple skin, my heart sighed in the realization that this was, indeed, a picture of timeless love that a thousand words would never begin to describe.

A wordsmith with no words, yet immeasurably content.

As I watched your exquisite form rise and fall with serene calmness in my arms, I stopped searching for words and smiled, choosing instead to relish the beauty of the scene unfolded ...

Of just how perfect this was – this stolen moment of joy.

My happiness spread from a single smile to a complete contentment as I finally understood.

Mate of my soul, friend of my spirit, love of my heart, you gave substance to the words I could always find before ...

You showed me what all the descriptions I had so long dreamed about actually meant ... and felt like.

I knew at that moment what I had never previously grasped.

Instead of dazzling words that failed to have meaning, I would trade all those wonderful tales and poems for this experience instead:

A moment, a lifetime with a love meant for me that defied description because words alone would never suffice.

The best love stories are beyond the pages, for they are told by the heart ...

And in your embrace, I felt every story, song and sonnet all fused into that cocoon of our love.

Happily ever after begins in your heart and
lasts beyond lifetimes in your soul.
As I kissed your lips, lingering inches away lost
in your eyes, I finally understood the meaning
of forever.

A familiar song came on the radio, and my heart almost fell apart.

A solitary tear rolled down my cheek as the words to a song that was once ours burned deeply into my soul.

All the memories of our love came rushing back, and I couldn't help but smile. The laughter we shared, the deep love we had, and the times of joy are something I'll always cherish.

For a time, our love story was magical, and it felt like we would be forever ...

But that's not how our story would go.

Somewhere along the way, we lost ourselves and stopped loving each other the way we deserved.

I know I played my part and didn't do all I could have done ... some love just isn't meant to last.

Everywhere I go, something reminds me of you – a restaurant, a song, even a TV show can trigger thoughts and feelings of you.

The wounds are fresh, and my heart still hurts, but I'm trying to move on ...

My head tells me that I have to start living for me again.

My heart tells me that there is still another chapter to our story and to not give up completely, but I'm trying not to listen.

I know I have to let go – and I will – but I know it won't happen until my heart is done grieving. Some say you stop loving someone once it falls apart, but I know I'll always have a special place in my heart for you ...

Nothing will ever change that.

Just because we're not together doesn't mean I don't think of you or wonder how you're doing ... it just means I'm not part of your life anymore ... and that I'm choosing my own path now.

I lie in bed at night lost in thoughts and memories, alternating between happiness and sadness ... and sleep can be so fleeting for me as my mind won't shut off.

I know I'll get through this and get over you, but I also know it's going to take time ... time for me to let go of the hurt, to find my own closure and to accept the fact that life is different now. Part of me wishes we would work things out, but I know that's not what I truly need.

I need to stand alone, find my strength and begin loving myself in the ways I stopped when we were together ... and it will be the hardest thing I've ever had to do.

So, as the song we once loved fades away, so do the thoughts of you.

I tell myself what's meant to be will always find a way, so I'm letting go.

It'll be hard for a while, but I also know it'll get easier.

It may take a long time, but I'll get there.

Day by day, step by step ... that's how I'm living my life now.

Finding small joys in the little things that make me smile.

I'll get to where I need to be, eventually.

Knowing that I will, for me for now, will have to be enough.

I can do this.

I Want To Set My Soul on Fire

I don't want a lackluster life or an ordinary love
… I need so much more than that.
I want to burn with the intensity of red-hot
passion or not at all ...
Passion for life, love and all the things that fill
my soul.
I want to experience everything in this life that
can't be found in a book or seen on a screen.
I want to feel the grass between my toes as I
close my eyes and the warm wind gusts
through my hair.
I want to hear the sweet laughter of happy child
nearby and the quiet whispers of lovers
cuddled up.
I want to feel the wet nose of a cute puppy and
the rain of a warm summer shower falling onto
my face.
The sweet smell of a blooming spring day and
the chirping of crickets on a muggy summer
night … that's what I love ... that's what my
heart craves.
The dancing fireflies that light up the twilight on
a cool fall day reminds me –this is why I am
alive.

I yearn to taste the fiery singe of love's passionate kiss often and run my fingers across my partner's skin.

I don't care about the ordinary choices that occupy the time of everyone else ...

No, give me the intensity of living in the moment and leaving no act undone nor any words left unsaid.

Leave the boring, dull and commonplace for others, I need the moments that set my soul on fire.

My road will lead me into uncharted waters that others have missed and places that are off the beaten path.

I want to know those feelings and sensations that make me feel alive, every day.

I want to lie in wonder under the pallid glow of a waning moon; I want to plunge headfirst into the beautiful splendor of the night sky.

I want to kiss endlessly, love recklessly and live truthfully.

I won't have a bucket list because I'll have done everything that I have ever yearned to experience.

My legacy won't be one of possessions, things or valuables, but of feelings, memories and fulfilled dreams.

I'll be the smile you never forget, the courage you never doubt and the heart that you never stop believing in.

I'll never be just a spark, a flame or a light.

I'll be a wildfire that sets your life on fire.

To feel my essence is to experience the burning sensation of being alive ...

truly energized in a way that fills every day, every moment with vigor.

I want to leave this place in such a way that with my last breaths I can say,

"I gave this life everything."

With love in my heart, and wonder in my soul, I'll spend the rest of my days exploring everything this world has to offer.

That's a little slice of the magic I keep tucked away in my spirit and will never relinquish ...

And you're never too old to stop believing in magic.

Unquenchable passion and intense desire – that's how I live my life and enjoy my days.

No stone unturned, no words left unspoken, no dream unchased.

I don't want ordinary, average or almost.
I want to burn in the fires of a red-hot love,
each and every day ...
And I want it all with you.
Let's go lose ourselves in the endless passion
of forever ...
Truly alive, happy and free.

I know they always told you that the real
strength is in holding on, and in some cases,
that's true.
But what if I told you that most of the time
letting go is the true strength?
That pain that you've been carrying with you all
this time ... holding onto it is not making you
stronger.
The pain from a breakup, childhood hurt, the
way someone treated you, when someone
made you feel not good enough ... that's been
tearing you apart for far too long.
You've been burying that your entire life, and
it's done nothing but bring you down and cause
you more anguish ...
Yes,
I'm talking to you.
You're right that no one will ever know those
roads you once traveled and the pain you had
to endure ...
But it's time to stop carrying those angry
feelings and guilt with you wherever you go.

True, you may never understand why someone mistreated you or hurt you, but you can't worry about that anymore.

Every minute you spend dwelling on things you couldn't control is time you're not healing.

Yes, I know it's hard to let go of the memories, the pain and the feelings of selflessness ...

And while you should never forget where you've been, you deserve better than to let them continue to destroy you.

You're more than enough – don't you dare let anyone tell you that you're not amazing, beautiful and worthy of the best that life has to offer.

Once you start opening your eyes and heart to the beauty of life all around you, you'll start to see more wonderful things happening to you.

I know it's going to hurt and you're still going to have sleepless nights, but you'll find that the more you begin to let go, the lighter your burden will feel.

Truth is, you may never really understand why they hurt you, and you have to be okay with that.

All that negative energy and those ugly feelings of resentment, guilt and shame are slowly eating away at your soul.

Take back your power and wrest control of your life and your joy from those things that live in your past.

I'm not saying you have to forget them, because the scars they left have created the beautifully unique person that is you.

Never regret the roads you've traveled nor the people you've loved –

Every one of them taught you something before they left ...

It's up to you to learn their lesson and let go of their pain.

Honestly, I don't know what tomorrow holds and sometimes, I don't even know how we'll get there ... but we will, together.

You're not alone.

Throw off the shackles of the painful past that have been weighing you down, and you'll discover your wings have been there all along, just waiting for you to learn to fly.

Yes, it's going to hurt and you're going to cry, but not for the same reasons you once did.

Take back your power and find your strength
… rise from those ashes that you've been
carrying with you for far too long.

Turn the page.

Begin a new chapter.

Write a new story.

Maybe your tale was once a montage of pain,
sadness and guilt, but not anymore.

This chapter, this new beginning is a story of
rising from the fire, letting go of the past and
starting to finally live again.

You've been down for too long.

It's time to start rising.

It's not enough to simply discover your wings ...
You must find the courage to fly.

Listen to the Voice That Tells You You're Worthy

I used to listen to the opinions of everyone I crossed paths with –
Of who I was, what I should be and even what I should wear.
I tried and tried to fit into all the boxes that I thought would make everyone love me ...
And the funny thing is, it was never enough.
Every change I made just led to more criticisms and even more opinions.
Trying to fit in was a never-ending battle for approval and acceptance that I realized I could never win.
They liked to point out my flaws and imperfections, highlighting all the things I didn't like about myself.
At the end of the day, I was unhappy, unfulfilled and a nervous wreck.
I realized that I could spend my life trying to please people that I didn't really care about in ways that didn't matter for reasons that didn't make sense.
Or I could embrace my own unique qualities: scars, scratches, flaws and all.

And that my people would accept me just the way I am.

I realized that chasing the attention and affection of the people who pretended to be perfect would be a never-ending struggle ...

That I would never be happy trying to be something I wasn't.

So, I did what was long overdue ...

I stopped living for everyone else and starting living for myself.

I had spent so many years defining myself by others that I really didn't know who I was anymore.

It's hard to start a journey without a map ... but I knew that's what needed to happen if I were ever to be truly happy.

I had to find my joy and learn to love myself for all the things the world said I should be ashamed of ...

Truth is, the scars, the bumps and bruises that make me who I am aren't the bad parts of me ...

Just the opposite.

I'm finally understanding those are the things about me that I should celebrate, for they make me unique in a way that an easy life never would have.

So, yes, I've made mistakes, fallen down and chosen to love the wrong people ...

But I'm growing, I'm learning and I'm finally starting to love all of myself – even the parts that everyone said I should hide.

I'm flawsome, I'm a mess sometimes and I may not know where I'll be tomorrow, and I'm okay with that.

I'm living my life the way I choose, and no one can take that away from me.

It may not be easy, but I'm owning my experiences and finally listening to my heart.

It took me a long time, but I know now what I never did before.

I'm worth it, I'm awesome and I deserve to be happy ...

In just the way I want.

The Peace I Have Now Is Worth Everything I Lost When You Left

When I lost you, I thought I'd never be happy again.
For so long, you were all I could think of and every happy thought or memory was tied to you.
I buried the pain from what happened between us and tried to distance my heart so that I could try to stop hurting, eventually ...
And truthfully, I really didn't know if the anguish would ever subside.
It seemed that all I could focus on was losing you and the sadness that caused ... But when I began looking for hope, something miraculous happened ...
I found myself instead.
All the things I had lost in us, all the parts of me that vanished as I tried to make you happy ...
they slowly started to reappear.
I had spent so much time chasing you or vying for your attention that I had stopped doing the things that made my soul happy.
Incredibly, every day that passed ...
I rediscovered a little more of myself.

With those remembered pieces, the pain began to subside slowly ... a bit more each day ... until finally, the hurt was much like you – a distant memory of a time and a feeling that couldn't hurt me anymore.

When you walked away from me, I thought I had lost everything, and the funny thing is, just the opposite happened.

I found it all instead – everything that mattered and that I had needed all along:

My happiness, my peace and most of all, my love for myself.

You gave me the greatest gift of all by letting me go ... you pointed the way back to me.

And now, I'm never looking back.

I've got no interest in living in the past and revisiting the pain ... there's nothing there for me now.

I found a love in my heart and a peace in my soul ... and it was because of me, not you.

It's strange, really, that the end of our relationship wasn't really the end at all.

It was the beginning of everything good that I needed to find again –

I had been lost for too long, but not anymore.

I'm on my way back home now.

Thank goodness for the broken roads that led
me to exactly where I was always meant to be.

I stopped trying to be everyone's favorite flavor
a long time ago.

Everyone knows what they like, and my spice
isn't always a popular preference ... And that's
okay with me.

It took me a lot of years and hurt feelings to
understand that I can't please the world ...

So, I stopped trying.

I spent too much time trying to impress the
people that didn't matter in ways that weren't
real ... and it was exhausting.

I was never going to fit into a label, box or fake
definition of something I would never be.

This is my life, and no one knows the path I've
walked.

So, I stopped trying to be all the things I was
never meant to be.

My happiness, my self-respect and my self
love are more valuable to me than any amount
of approval will ever be.

They can keep their need to approve, accept
and judge me ... what they think will never
change who I am.

They don't know me.
In fact, most never will.
My people – the ones who love me – they get me, and I get them.
They accept and love me unconditionally for who I am ...
So, everyone else can find someone else to judge, because I don't care what the world thinks of me.
I spend my time and energy being kind, loving and respectful ...
But I'm also saucy, sassy and colorful ...
And that's too much for some people.
That's their loss.
I'll never again try to be a people pleaser because the only opinion that matters is my own.
I'll keep being the best person I can be, with character and dignity, and that's all I can do.
Keep working to improve me.
The world has plenty of fake people following the crowd pretending to be something they will never be for reasons that don't matter.
They can keep that nonsense.
Maybe I'm flawed, maybe I'm a mess at times.

But at least I'll always be true to who I am and real to the people I meet.
My heart is gold, not gold-plated and my soul is deep, not shallow.
My life, my way ...
Beautiful in all the ways that matter to me.

The Woman Who Won't Take Disrespect From Anyone

The men would call her a firecracker and praise her strong demeanor, saying they loved a woman like her ...
Until they realized they couldn't tame her or make her acquiesce to their wishes.
They'd chase her, woo her and try to impress her with the things that she didn't care about ...
Because they didn't understand her at all.
And that was fine with her.
They had an agenda that she found amusing, and it frustrated them when they realized that she saw past their facades ...
She didn't need a man, love or anyone trying to pretend to be something they weren't.
She knew all the people who praised her strength didn't really know what it meant to be strong.
She wasn't that way because she wanted to be – life had left her no choice ...
But she didn't care about the opinion of those who didn't know a thing about the fires she'd survived.

That same courage and saucy personality that the weaker men claimed to admire would be the one thing they could never handle.

She knew who she was and where she was going and all the fake admiration from people with ulterior motives meant nothing to her.

Yes, she was strong ...

But she was so much more than that.

She was deep, soulful, loving and passionate in ways the rest of them would never comprehend.

She lived and loved honestly and without regret, for she owned her scars and appreciated her imperfections.

She didn't have anything to prove to anyone and those that tried to judge her?

She just walked away from them without uttering a word ... she was better than that.

She'd never stoop to win the affection of those who didn't really care about her – only what they could get from her, and she had neither the time nor the patience to deal with those types.

She was happy with the life she chose, and she kept her walls high to fend off all the

imposters intent on trying to love her in selfish ways.
She'd just keep walking past the pretenders, the followers and would-be lovers ...
Smiling, sassing and laughing every step of the way.
She knew they'd never realize just how amazing she truly was ...
And until someone came along that did,
She'd just keep shining bright like the diamond she was.

He knows she's lost faith in love, that she doesn't believe that things work out for anyone, not anymore.

But he can see past the high walls she's built to protect herself; he sees her distant but beautiful soul that just wants to be loved ... In all the ways she loves her people: Passionately, honestly, faithfully and respectfully.

He feels her distrust and distance from the very first glance, and he knows why ... All the ones before him told her they would never leave, but they always did.

He knows he must be patient, understanding and empathetic to really connect with the wonderful woman behind those placid eyes.

She can't change who she is – she has done whatever it took to rebuild herself after every heartbreak and letdown ... and he realizes that.

Taking her hand, he holds it to his mouth and slowly kisses it, looking at her with every ounce of bare truth he can muster.

"I can't promise I'll be perfect or that I'll never make mistakes … but I can promise to love and appreciate you every day in the way you have always deserved ... Starting with today."

He wiped away the solitary tear streaming down her face, smiling warmly.

Nodding nervously, her voice cracked as she spoke.

"All I want is to love and be loved in a way that I've always wanted … can you do that?"

He beamed and pulled her close to him, embracing her firmly, their bodies meshing as one.

"Yes, my love, I can … and I will."

Looking back, they would both always remember that moment when their lives changed irrevocably ...

The time when two became one and their love became real.

He understood and appreciated her one most intimate truth:

While the most broken women have the highest walls,

They also have the deepest love.

There were so many times I didn't think I would make it ...
When I thought heartbreak, life or failure would finally overwhelm me.
The days when everything that could go wrong did, and it took everything I had just to keep going.
People would tell me I'm strong, brave or whatever word they chose to use ...
I just called it survival.
I didn't have the answers and I rarely knew the way; all I knew for sure was that I couldn't quit.
Underneath the misery and past the darkness in my life was a flickering light that kept calling to me ...
It would whisper to me amidst my struggle, "Don't give up."
Every time I wanted to throw in the towel, each time I thought I was done,
I would think of that distant light and muster up the courage to pick myself up, dust myself off and press forward.

It was painful and hard, never without strife and struggle, but I always found my way.

There were times when lived in a constant state of fear – holding my breath waiting for the next bad thing, heartache or disappointment.

That's a tough place to be – always expecting disaster around every corner.

I got to a point where I just got tired ... tired and fed up.

I was sick of living my life fighting for survival every day, holding onto the painful past and thinking that what I was doing would change my present or future.

All the anger, shame and guilt of where I'd been were burning me like a branding iron ... Searing the fear into my psyche that I couldn't shake, shackling me and weighing me down so heavily I could barely smile.

I hit that wall and something inside of me clicked.

I was done living afraid of what might happen, who might hurt me or what could go wrong.

It would take a long journey and many battles, but I was determined to change my mindset, lighten my heart and free my soul.

Looking back now, I realize that choice saved my life, because my downward spiral would have consumed me whole.

Maybe I don't have the answers or even know where I'm going some days, but I know I'll end up where I'm meant to be.

I found that distant light that was calling to me for so long … it was the love for myself that was just waiting to be found.

So, yes, I started over, stumbled and fell ... But I also rose again, dug myself out and found my wings.

My life isn't perfect and won't ever be,
But with love in my heart and peace in my soul,
I'm living my life and finding my love just the way I was always meant to.
For me, by me, because of me.
Beautiful, strong and free.

A Stranger Where Once There Was a Soulmate

I can't help but cry when I look at you now,
wondering where we went wrong ...
Hurting as I try to understand what went wrong.
It's hard when someone who was once so
close slowly becomes a stranger.
I don't know where we lost our way or how we
fell apart, but little pieces of my heart shattered
every time we drifted further away from each
other.
There was a time when our connection was
powerful, and your love was so strong that I
thought nothing could ever tear us asunder.
I couldn't have been more wrong, and now I
just don't know what to do with these feelings
of loss ...
I don't know what emotion to feel first:
Regret, sadness, anger ... so many visceral
emotions wash over me about us.
As we have slowly stopped being close, it feels
as though I have lost a little part of myself
along the way.

I can't pick a time or place that caused us to become strangers, but I cry when I don't see the person I once knew behind your eyes.

This may be the hardest thing I've ever had to face, and the worst part is that I'm dealing with it alone.

I used to know everything you were thinking and all your heart's desires from just a single glance ... and now, nothing.

I once held your heart in my hands and your soul whispered to mine every day ...

And it's been so long since I've heard your soul that I don't even think I know you anymore.

I can't say if it's because you chose to hide from me, you don't care, or something happened ... I may never know.

I don't know if love can die, but I know some feelings can slowly fade away ... and it's so heartbreaking that our love has dissipated into so very little ... almost an apathy that tears my heart in two.

I wish I had the answers or knew what to do to fix us, but my heart tells me it's too far gone ... you're too far away now.

How did we ever go from lovers to strangers? Where did you lose your love for me and why?

As I close my eyes and try to hold onto the memories of the good times, I exhale forcibly and fight to hold myself together ... And it takes every ounce of strength I have not to break down into tears.

Everything that's fallen apart – us, what's happened – it all just makes me sad.

Maybe we will find our way back to each other, but I can't hope for that any longer ... I can't live trying to pin my heart onto dreams and possibilities anymore.

I have to stay in those places where I can hold onto happiness, because memories are all that I have left of us now.

Maybe your soul will find mine once again in the darkness, but for now, that's just a fading dream and one that seems so far away.

I don't know what tomorrow will bring, but I can't think about the future right now.

I will live fully in the moments, find the beauty where I can and appreciate what I have.

It's sad that my happy thoughts come from the past now, but sooner or later, I'll have to move on.

I only hope and pray that you remember what we had before it's too late.

Either way, I'm doing what I have to do to be happy again … with or without you.
Today, I'm going to start living for myself again.
I'm taking back my magic, my life and my happiness …
One day,
One smile,
And one dream at a time.

I told you when we met that I was different from all the others.

Now you know exactly what I meant.

I'm not trying to be difficult, unique or challenging. Far from it.

I'm just me … and that's too much for some people.

That's their loss.

Some call me a handful, stubborn or hard to love, but that's just because they're not up to the task.

I'll never tell you that I don't have my challenges and baggage because everyone does.

I own who I am and where I've been, and those unique imperfections and chaotic beautiful things about me …

Those are just part of my package.

My scars tell my story, and it's a tale of courage and charisma, failure and flight, but most of all, it's about love.

A real and authentic love for my people, loyal and beautiful every day.

I live my life unapologetically and bravely, unafraid to take chances and stand out from the crowd.

I've had my heart broken like so many others have, but I never dwelled on what went wrong or why it didn't work.

I just learned from every mistake and evolved from each failed relationship.

No, I'm not easy to love, and I realize that I'm a complete mess some days.

I cry suddenly for no reason and I snort at bad jokes, but we both know that's charming.

Sure, my hair is a disaster most of the time and I sometimes forget what I'm doing while I'm doing it … but I just chalk that up to my beautiful quirks.

I'm not going to ask or beg you to love me, but if you think you have what it takes, then step up, man up, and let's go get lost in some adventure.

I'm not for the faint of heart and I'll never be your "maybe" girl,

You're either all in with me or I'm out.

I don't believe in halfway love and I'm never going to accept anything less than what I deserve … which is your best.

So, I'm putting out there exactly who I am and what I want ...
I'm beautiful in the ways that matter, and I'm passionately loving all the time.
I'm deep and I'm soulful.
I'm the wild rose you always wanted to find and love ...
The question is ...
Can you handle my thorns?

When Our Lips Meet and Souls Connect, Nothing Else Matters

In that instant when our lips meet, there ceases to be a me or you, only a "we" without ending … two bodies without separation, two souls fused into one, two hearts beating singularly. The air I breathe is ours, this love we have found is without equal.
In this moment, when we meet, souls colliding, hearts unifying and spirits melting into one … Passions' reckoning unending.
The world dissipates and time stands still … the cocoon of our love tucking us away from all else, because in those stolen moments, we are all that matters.
Our love is all that I know …
All that I feel, need and want … nothing else.
If my life and love held but a solitary truth, it would have a name, a face, a meaning … It would, always has been,
and always will be … you.

You look at me and all you can see is what's different about me.

I know I don't fit into your definition of normal, and I've long since accepted who I am.

I love every imperfection and challenge that is part of my life.

When you only see what makes me unique, you stop seeing me as the person that I am ...

And begin to view me for all the things that set me apart.

You forget that I have feelings, emotions and thoughts like everyone else.

That's okay, though.

I'm always going to shine brightly because that's what I've decided I want to do.

I'll never accept anyone's limitations of who they think I am, and I'll always shine from within because I can do anything if I decide to.

Don't tell me what I can't do because I've been climbing mountains since the very beginning.

I don't know how to quit, and I'll never forget who I am and what I'm capable of.

I didn't get to choose the things that set me apart, but I do choose how to live my life.

So, please stop trying to label me – to fit me into what you think I should be – and just accept me as I am.

I don't seek anything that you wouldn't want for yourself.

Respect, courtesy and kindness … and I'll give much more than that in return.

I'm genuine, I'm real and yes, I'm special – but in a beautiful way that I love about myself.

I'm not saying my life is easy or that it doesn't have challenges,

I just ask that you take my hand, walk with me and appreciate who I am.

Maybe you don't understand my past or the road that I've traveled to get where I am, but you can love me for my flaws and treat me with kindness.

Rise or fall, rain or shine, I'm always going to remain true to who I am ...

I may not always be everyone's favorite flavor, but they'll always know what they're getting when they meet me.

I love who I am and where I'm going, but the question I have is this –

Can you accept and love me for me ...

Just as I am?

People will ask me how I succeed and keep
going and to share my secret ...

I'll just look at them and smile.

I'll give them the nondescript answer that I
know they want to hear, like "hard work,"
because very few of them want the reality of
how I've made it to where I am.

They think I was given opportunities and just
made it work.

They couldn't be any more wrong.

I wasn't given anything, not even a chance by
most people.

I started below the lowest rung and dug myself
out of the pit of failure.

Back then, I didn't have wings – I didn't even
know what those were.

No, I had claws.

I had to scrap, fight and find a way to survive,
fight back and overcome all the adversity that
tried to bring me down.

It wasn't easy, it always hurt and there were so
many times I thought I'd never make it.

But each time, I dug deep into my faltering
courage and pulled myself out of the darkness.

Whether it was a broken heart, a career disaster or a personal meltdown, it seemed like life was always trying to make me quit ...

Because it was.

But you see, that's the thing about me ...

I don't know how to quit; I'm not wired to stay down.

I can fall to my knees, I can struggle and fail, but eventually, I'm going to find my strength and way out of whatever brought me down.

No one gave me a chance and I never asked for help.

I knew who I was and what I could do, so I didn't need an opportunity ...

I made my own breaks.

I forged a stronger spirit with each fire that threatened to tear me apart, and I became braver each time I stepped off the ledge.

I stopped being afraid of what would happen, and I started believing that I could do it.

It all came down to me.

I survived but then I thrived.

I failed but then I learned.

I stumbled but then I grew.

I arose and then I found my wings.

So, when they ask me what I owe my success to, there's really only one answer that matters to me.

I owe it all to myself.

I wouldn't change a thing about where I've been or where I'm going because I'm right where I'm supposed to be.

I still have bad days and days when I don't want to leave the house.

Those are the times that I just find a way to keep going and make sure to show up.

Maybe I won't be famous or rich, but I'll be happy knowing that I did it all how I always wanted to ...

My way.

She knew that he was wrong for her from the very beginning – bad boys usually are – but it didn't stop her from getting sucked into his world.

His passion and ferocity overwhelmed her senses in a way she'd never known.

But deep down, she knew the truth.

He wasn't going to be tied down, and she'd be chasing a ghost ... so, she did the only thing she could and let him go.

It was one of the hardest things she'd ever had to do, but she knew it was necessary if she wanted to salvage the self-respect she had left.

It had been a whirlwind romance, a combination of desire and passion that swept her off her feet.

She tried to tell herself it was fleeting – just an affair – but her heart whispered that it was more.

She shook her head defiantly.

It didn't matter what she wanted to believe, she had to fight her heart and listen to her judgement ...

A woman's intuition is rarely wrong.

She craved him in a way that was wholly unfamiliar to her, and she knew letting him go would be one of the hardest things she had ever done.

But she was resolute and strong.

He would chase her, she knew, but for all the wrong reasons ... and she needed someone to chase her for the right ones.

She knew that everyone comes into your life for a reason, a season or a lifetime, and she was thankful they had crossed paths.

He had shown her what true passion was and now, she wouldn't settle for anything less.

As she started her car and slumped back in the seat, tears came streaming down her face.

She'd miss him, she knew, but these would the last tears she would shed for him.

She needed and deserved more – he was unapologetically who he was and part of her loved him for it.

She was incredibly attracted to his fierce passion and alpha presence ... but she was a complex woman who also needed soul, love and depth.

She shook her head. When your heart wages against your head – when what you think you opposes what you know is best – that's the hardest fight of all.

But, if love can fade, then so can pain.

She drove away and she never looked back.

She moved on and evolved.

Smiling, she wiped the tears from her eyes.

She knew it would get harder before it would get easier, but she was strong enough to see it through.

And she knew she would come out better and stronger for it.

Because while he had shown her true passion, he would never be able to give her everything she truly needed, and she deserved to be happy … in all of the ways she wanted without exception or compromise ...

Now and for always.

She realized that he was different from the first
glance.
The way he moved, the way he spoke,
The way his gaze penetrated her soul.
She was so used to explaining herself to all the
men she'd loved before ...
She was stunned when he just understood her
without a word said.
She didn't know what to say or how to act
having her soul bared before a man ...
It was deathly frightening,
But it was beautiful in a way that eclipsed
words.
Moreover, she didn't try to hide or pretend
because she didn't have to.
He just got it, he accepted and appreciated her
... all of her ... and that was something she'd
never known.
Unconditionally and devotedly.
She was so used to kissing all the frogs hoping
for a prince that she was speechless to finally
meet the one that she knew was meant to be
hers.

She tried to deny the connection and guard her heart, but it was no use.

She had yearned for this moment, this love, for so long that she was dumbfounded as it had found her so unexpectedly ... but without a shadow of a doubt, with complete and utter certainty, she knew he was the one.

So familiar, she felt as though they had loved each other for countless lifetimes before ... and perhaps they had.

She just had this feeling that she had always known him.

As she nestled into him, her heart sighed and her soul felt at ease for the first time in, well, ever.

"This is what home feels like," she thought as she looked up at him.

Her voice cracked as she whispered, their eyes meeting as she spoke.

"I missed you, long before I ever met you."

He smiled and kissed her forehead.

Stroking her hair, he spoke the words she had waited a lifetime to hear.

"I'm just sorry it took me so long to find you, but I'm here now. Let's enjoy the rest of forever. I love you."

She sighed and burrowed deeper into his chest.

This was worth waiting a hundred lifetimes for, and she would cherish every moment of their love story just the way she had always wanted to be loved.

Meant to be will always find a way,
Just as it had for her that one beautiful day.

Light Has a Way of Finding Those Who Seek It

I know you've been hurt so many times you
don't want to believe in love anymore.
You've built the highest walls around your
heart because you've promised yourself that
you're done getting hurt.
You've cried so many tears for people who just
left you without caring at all ...
And that's their loss.
If they don't know your value, then you're
better off without them.
The right people – your people – will always
love and appreciate you just the way you are.
You don't have to change, sacrifice or settle
when it comes to the people you're meant for.
I know you've convinced yourself that love isn't
real and that there's no one out there for you ...
but you're wrong.
The voices of doubt whisper in your soul that
you're damaged and that no one will want you.
Stop listening because that's not true.
You are an amazing and loving person who
needs to learn how to love again ...
Starting with yourself.

Stop dwelling in the darkness and step out into the light ... let your beautiful soul shine.

The world needs more lights like you.

Stop selling yourself short and believing you aren't good enough because you're more than enough.

I know you have every reason not to believe it can get better, that you'll find love or even that you'll be happy one day. I'm telling you that I believe in you and that you can ... and will.

Find the light within and seek the love for yourself that you lost along the way.

You've been fighting for so long just trying to survive, I'm telling you to start wanting more.

You deserve to be cherished.

Start living ... one day at a time.

Find the small joys in your life, notice the beauty all around you and hold the love in your life close to your heart, because it's there, waiting for you to find it.

You forgot your magic and how to love yourself when you got beaten down by life. That stops now.

If you don't believe in you, then take my hand and listen to my words ... I believe in you.

You can do whatever you set your mind to ...
baby steps, small victories and uncovering
your self love.

When you awaken the forgotten parts of your
heart and soul, your life will start to slowly
change ... one small blessing at a time. After
all, love finds you in its own time when you're
ready and receptive, and not one minute
before.

This is your story, so turn the page and start
again. You can't rewrite the beginning, but you
can start a new chapter.

You hold the pen, and it's magical, my dear.
What are you waiting for?

Life, love and happiness are waiting for you.
Take my hand.

Let's go find some magic.

Sometimes Doing What's Right Is the Hardest Choice

I look at my phone as your name pops up, and I sigh deeply. It's a hard place to be when you know what you must do but your heart isn't totally ready to let go.

My mind has been screaming at me to move on for some time, a little bit louder with each fight or sleepless night.

I know what's best for me, and I have for some time, but love is a hard thing to ignore and just walk away from ... that's where I'm stuck.

I gave us my all – being there through all the hard times and standing strong through the bad days – but sometimes, I felt like I was standing alone. I tried to talk to you, share with you how I felt so that we could work through our problems and get back to loving each other the way we could ... but you never really wanted to talk, you were always too busy and made me feel like it didn't matter to you.

Well, it mattered to me. We mattered to me. I guess I was the only one who felt that way. You've broken my heart a little more every day with your apathy and hurtful words.

It's sad, but I've just hit that wall where my heart can't take any more. I've got to take my happiness out of your hands because you've not really cared about that for a while … and that's what hurts worst of all.

I just needed something – anything – from you to keep fighting for us, but I guess that was asking for too much.

Shame on you for making me believe that you wanted a future with me when we were fresh and new, and shame on me for holding on when you weren't even willing to put in the work.

It takes two people working together for a successful relationship, and that's something that I don't know that you'll ever understand … or maybe you just don't even care.

It really doesn't matter anymore.

My self-respect and self love are all I have left, and I'm done fighting for us ... I'm fighting for me now instead.

Maybe I'll look back one day with regret, but it will only be with the wish that things had gone differently and that you had met me halfway. That you had tried to make us work.

I did what I could do, and I'll move on knowing that I gave us our all.

Some people were meant to stay in our hearts, not in our lives.

I wish you the best, I'll never forget the time we had and the love we shared, but I've grown from this and learned more about myself ... it won't be easy, and I'll still think about you from time to time.

But as I decide not to answer your call, I'm making the choice to move on and focus on me.

I'm working on loving myself more now.

What's meant to be will always find a way, so I know I'll end up where I'm supposed to be.

Wherever that is, at least I'll be happy again.

That, for now, will have to be enough.

Happy, free and at peace ... finally.

A Vow To Love Myself

I've survived some pretty bad stuff in my life –
things I never thought I would make it through.
I scrapped, I clawed, and I fought my way past
all the flames of failure to reach deep and
discover the strength I didn't know I had.
When I was on my knees facing the abyss,
that's when I learned who I truly was and what
I am capable of.
I was never defined by the mistakes I made,
but by how strongly I arose after falling.
It's easy to love yourself when everything is
going right and doors are opening all around
you ... it's quite a different experience when
you're at your lowest.
I learned who was there for me and, most of
all, that there is beauty in the scars of my story.
Every scratch, bump and bruise remind me
where I've been and of the bridges I've burned
so that I would never go back
to those places that I should have never been.
I learned not only to love the parts of me that
once frustrated me, but I learned to celebrate
my imperfections, for they described my

broken beauty in a way that my words never could.

So, as I step out into today, you'll see a smile on my face and a spring in my step.

I've come a long way in my life, and I'm proud of the person I'm becoming.

It hasn't been easy, it hasn't been painless, and it's been slow ... but I've learned from every mistake and grown from every experience.

This is my story. It's a tale of disaster and failure, mistakes and falling ... but it's also a story of rising from the ashes, getting stronger and learning to love every scar of my broken beauty.

After all, the cracks are how the light gets in ... And now, I'm on fire for being alive.

I've taken a vow to love myself and that's just what I'm going to do, one day a time.

Beautifully broken and wonderfully imperfect ... just the way I was meant to be.

Some Steps Need To Be Taken Alone

I came to a place in my life where I realized I
needed to keep growing and evolving in a way
that made me happy.

I had depended on everyone to help me along
the way, but I've gone as far as I can with their
help ... I need to take the next steps on my
own.

To uncover who I really am and where I'm
supposed to be, I have to be brave enough to
go it alone.

I can't identify myself through love or my
friends anymore.

Even though those are big parts of my life, they
are only part of my story.

I'm turning the page and writing my tale of
personal growth with fire in my heart and hope
in my soul ... no one can go there for me.

It's scary when you step out alone into the
world, trying to find your wings when you've
never flown before.

But I can do this – flying high is more than just
finding your wings, it's also about having the
courage to try ... and I'm braver than I've ever

been, stronger than I've ever known, and I'll find my way.

I know the road ahead will have some bumps and bruises, but I'm ready for it ...

I've been ready my whole life, I just didn't always know it.

In order to be who I'm meant to be, I have to conquer this mountain on my own.

I'll always have the support of the people who love me, but this journey is for me to take by myself.

I can't hear the song in my heart if I'm surrounded by voices all around me.

It's the fires of struggle that forge my spirit to rise above ... and I've got this.

Maybe it'll take some time, it definitely won't be easy, but with passion in my soul and courage to fly high,

There's nothing I can't do.

I believe in me ... and that's a beautiful thing that no one can ever take away from me.

I don't know what tomorrow will bring, but if you look up, chances are, you'll see me flying high and burning brightly ...

That's who I am, beautiful and strong.

I'll figure it out,

Starting with today,
Starting with me ...
I'll finally discover who I was always meant to
be.

Don't Ask Me How I Survived, Ask Me What Song I Played on Repeat When I Thought My Whole World Was Over

If you want to truly know who I am, don't ask me about where I've been or the things I've seen or done.

I'll gladly share my journey with you – the wonders, the miracles and all the bad stuff in between.

But that doesn't begin to capture the true depths of my essence.

No, I'm not defined by where I've been or the struggles that shaped me ...

My soul is deeper and older than just places and things.

Ask me instead about the music that got me through the times when nothing else could.

The beautiful tapestry of lyrics and melodies that permeated my soul and instilled hope in my spirit.

Those feelings that inspired me to get up, dust myself off and rise again are the core of everything I am.

In fact, even now, I often find that music helps me find the words that escape me for my current triumph, mood or obstacle.

No matter how hard my day has been or where life has led me, the right song can transport me to a different place ...

One of happiness, hope and courage.

Maybe it's only for a few minutes, but in that precious time, I feel like I can do anything, be anything, conquer anything.

Those times in my life when I was at my lowest, I always had music ...

To lift me up, to help me breathe again, to remind me that everything was going to be okay.

My whole world could feel like it was ending, but there was always a song that could fill my soul with passion and help me through those struggles.

So, if you want to uncover my secrets and learn my truths, don't start with the ordinary adventures that just tell you where I've been.

Listen to the songs of my soul, and you'll forever understand ...

why music will always set me free.

I Need the Extraordinary

I tried my best to fit in, to conform and follow the crowd ... I just wasn't cut out to be like everyone else.

Try as I might, being a follower just didn't suit me.

I wasn't born to be mild and blend in with the ordinary and average.

I need more than the usual stuff and routine life.

Give me the people, places and things that fill my soul, the stuff that sparks my heart with vivid passion and fiery adventure.

I need the things that most people don't because I'm not like everyone else.

I did my best to settle for a 9-5 life with a cottage house and a white picket fence ... It just didn't take.

I need to be truly alive every day, to immerse myself into life in a way that few ever do ... to lose myself in the moments of beauty all around me and stimulate my passions to ride the wind.

Forget lackluster, boring and meek, I can't live without the zest of life calling my name.

It's more than just who I am, it's what my soul needs to feel alive.

Gorgeous music, wonderful places, colorful people … show me the way to undiscovered adventure.

I was never meant to be just another pretty face or average person; I was born to be free. Maybe you'd call me wild, irresponsible or flighty, but I'll tell you I'm spontaneous, intuitive and passionate.

I'm not for everyone, but my close circle, the people that really get me – they are the family that I choose that loves me without condition or judgement.

That's part of my magic, after all.

I have a huge heart, I embrace love for the people who earn my affection, and I'm always there for them.

I'm the person you can count on to whisk you off on a wild ride, to have your back when you need me and to celebrate your biggest victories.

You can always count on me to drag you off the beaten path, to do something unusual and maybe even a little scary in the best possible ways … that's who I am and always will be.

I don't want to simply exist ... I'm going to truly live life to the fullest every day.

Maybe I live by the seat of my pants, but I'm a free spirit and I'm just lovable that way.

I might not be your flavor ... but you'll never look past me when we meet.

Maybe you'll smile, maybe you'll shake your head,

But you'll never forget the most beautiful soul you've ever met.

That's just who I am and always will be.

Strong, wild and free.

People would look at her and marvel at her strong demeanor and powerful presence.

She didn't just enter a room, she owned it upon her arrival.

She was strong willed and fiery, the sort of woman who inspired other women and intimidated most men.

She didn't try to be anything unique or different, she just focused on being the best version of herself.

Confident, proud and defiant, her voice was unmistakable, and her opinion was always known.

Simply put, she was a force of nature who didn't take no for an answer and never quit.

But the thing most would never know about this strong and passionate woman was that she was much the same as most others – she had fears and insecurities, just like all the women around her.

The difference was, she didn't allow those demons to control who she was and how she lived.

She didn't give into the voices that tried to whisper in the dark that she wasn't enough, that she wouldn't make it.

No, she had been stuck in that dark place once and vowed never to return.

Not only had she failed, she had done so spectacularly … and everyone thought she was finished.

But that's the thing about strong and independent women … they don't know anything other than to get up and keep fighting.

She walked through the fires of her failures and emerged stronger, wiser and braver.

She didn't always have the answers or know the right way, but she believed in herself enough to know that she'd find her way.

She'd lose some, she'd win some, but she'd always do it with her own style and by her own choice.

She wasn't a one in a million woman, she was a once in a lifetime lady.

So, as the world watched her ascension with awe and admiration, she would just smile through the pain that fueled her fire.

She'd never forget where she'd been or who she was.

She was powerful not because she wasn't scared, but because she went on so strongly despite the fear.
She lived and loved with reckless abandon.
She was and always would be ...
The hero of her own story.

I'm Not the Fighter, I'm the Prize

I told you when we met that I don't play games,
but I guess you might need a little reminder.
I know the other ones before me were different
than me, but that's why you never wanted
them.
You're used to being in control of the
relationship, of your partner and getting
whatever you want ... but that's not going to fly
with me.
Real relationships are about communication,
respect and love.
I don't think you've ever really experienced true
love before, because you're used to everyone
giving you what you want how you want it.
I don't do that.
If you can't meet me halfway, and if you don't
know what unselfish love truly means, we
might have a problem.
I'm not saying you can't evolve or change, but I
can't make you want that.
Only you can want to be better.
So, I'm not going to fight for your attention, and
I'm never going to be just "one of your girls," so

it's time for you to make up your mind and decide what you want.

I will fight for you, for us, until the last breath leaves my lungs, but I will not fight to be important or for your attention … I know my worth and my value.

No one can diminish who I am just because they think they're more important.

I own who I am with all my flaws and imperfections … and while I may be a glorious disaster, I know I'm a catch.

So, let's stop the mind games and let's talk about real stuff: life, love and the future.

I'm done sitting around and waiting for you to make up your mind about what you want.

It's now or never, and I'm not backing down. So, either step up or step aside, I've got dreams to catch and a future to build.

I'm happy with who I am and where I'm going … it's up to you to decide if you're up to the task of loving me the way I deserve.

Having a healthy and happy relationship doesn't just happen, it takes work, communication and love.

I'm all in.

Question is, can you handle my truth?

I know you've had some rough times lately, but that's not who you are.

Yes, I'm talking to you.

That doesn't define you.

You've made some bad choices and been down the wrong roads, but that's just part of life.

You can choose to stay down, or you can decide you're done dwelling on the bad stuff of the past and you're moving on.

You can't change where you've been, but the future is yet to be written, so this is your opportunity to seize today.

You're not the same person you once were – you're not standing still and just surviving anymore.

You're done being stuck in what's happened and it's your time to grow ...

You know you've needed to evolve for some time, but now, this is your wake-up call.

You've got this.

You're changing, little by little and day by day.

You're better than you were yesterday and not as good as you'll be tomorrow.

Let go of yesteryear's baggage that is weighing you down so you can learn to fly free again.

Forgive the people you once knew, and most of all, forgive yourself.

You did the best you could with what you had.

That person who got hurt, made mistakes and failed badly is gone.

You're better, wiser and stronger now.

Own your life and take charge of the things that matter:

Love, friendships, career, your dreams ... everything

Nothing is impossible if you start to believe ... and I believe in you more than you'll ever know.

Embrace the new you in this new year and begin cultivating the transformation of you.

Stop surviving and just getting by. You're better than that.

Find your claws and dig yourself out of where you never should have been.

Unfurl your wings and start to fly again.

It's been so long since you've truly lived that you've forgotten who you are ... and you've lost your magic along the way.

So, yes, this is for you, this is that sign you've been searching for.

Don't tell me you can't or it's hopeless.

You're stronger than that. You can do this.

I won't tell you it'll be easy or painless, but it will definitely be worth it.

Awaken your soul, find your voice, stoke the passions of your heart.

You won't always know how to get there,

But I can promise you, you'll always end up exactly where you're meant to be.

So, take my hand and let's conquer today and all the days after.

If you can't find the courage and bravery to believe in yourself again, take some of mine, because I believe in you.

You'll figure it out, you'll find your way.

One day at a time and one step after another.

And one day, in the not-too-distant future, when you're soaring like you've always wanted, you'll look back and see me smiling at you, cheering you on.

And you'll finally understand what I've always known ... you were always capable of great things, you just needed to believe.

Now, it's your time to fly high, so keep going
and don't look back.
You've got a future to build ...
Starting with today,
Starting with you.

I Just Need Someone Who Won't Give Up When Loving Me Gets Hard

I told you when we met that I was a handful,
and I know you thought you could handle it, but
now I'm not so sure.
I always said I wasn't an easy one to love, but I
also said that I was worth the effort.
Yeah, I'm a complete mess most days, running
out the door doing my makeup and in a tizzy a
good bit of the time,
But that's just part of my unpredictable charm.
I never claimed to have it all figured out, but
that doesn't mean I don't love you with all my
heart.
I always love hard when there's love to be had,
that's probably one of the best things about me
...
I love deeply, honestly and passionately.
And while there's a lot of beautiful disaster that
comes with my big heart ...
it's never on purpose.
I know you don't understand me a lot of the
times, and truthfully, I don't get me sometimes
either.
But that's just part of my fun personality:

Unpredictable, loving and always awesome.
What more could you ask for?
Yes, I still cry randomly in the car when I get
stressed out and I say "I'm fine" when I'm
anything but okay.
I can't deny I have my moments.
But I deserve someone who can fight for me,
stand beside me through the hard times, and
hold my hand when things are tough.
I'm not going to pretend I'm a walk in the park,
because I'm not.
But I'm loyal, I'm real and I'm always there for
you when you need me.
I'll never give up on us, and I'm loyal to a fault,
but it takes both of us to make this work.
So, I guess you have a choice to make
because I've made my feelings known for
some time.
If you don't have what it takes to love me the
way I deserve, do us both a favor and let's part
ways amicably.
We both deserve to be happy, and if you're
going to keep giving up on us, then I'm better
off alone ...
At least I know what to expect when I'm
depending on myself.

I don't need to be saved, fixed or completed.

I just need to be loved, appreciated and respected ...

So, if you're down for that, let's keep building a future and chasing our dreams.

If not, let me go.

Either way, I'll be just fine ...

I always am.

I may be difficult, but I'm also strong.

And this, too, shall pass.

Tomorrow is another day full of possibilities ...

It's just a question of whether or not you'll be a part of it.

Can you stand the rain?

Where has the romance gone?
When did so many of us stop being gentlemen
and ladies?
How ever did character, class and courage
stop being of utmost importance?
Why did we stop opening doors and being
respectful, start disrespecting each other ...
and think that was okay?
We cherish the songs that touch our hearts, yet
we don't act with honor and class.
How did chivalry begin to die, and why is
morally decrepit behavior becoming the new
acceptable standard?
I want to see a movement back to the things
that matter: deep soulful love and passionate
living ... the kind that sets your heart on fire.
So many don't fight for love anymore when
times get tough, they just look for a
replacement.
When did quitting on vows of "'til death do us
part" become commonplace?
Let's start finding a way to make it work instead
of looking for an easy out.
Respect her, love her, cherish her.

Be loyal to him, care about him, listen to him.
Stop the deceit, disrespect and dishonor.
Less disappearing and more communicating.
There are some things in this life worth fighting for, and if you truly love someone, fight for them not against them.
It's okay to fight for someone you love, it's not okay to make someone fight to love you.
Don't let go just because the world knocks you down ... life will bring you to your knees if you let it, but you don't have to stay down.
Lean on each other and hold each other's hands through the storms.
Stand up stronger together.
Don't let true romance be the ideals of a time past, but instead the promise of a generation to come.
Maybe I'm old fashioned, but I know there's hope enough out there to rekindle the courage of chivalry and the authenticity of romance.
Don't ask yourself where has the class gone ... become the class.
Don't wait for an example to show you how to elevate your thinking and behavior,
Set the standard by being a light for others to follow.

Be the person that leads by example and the rest will fall into place.

We can't expect to find our fairy tales if we aren't willing to step up and be the hero and heroine.

Be different. Be passionate.

Be brave and act on your feelings.

Tell them how you feel, then show it.

Be romantic, be respectful.

Listen to your heart ... then act on it.

Every day.

Fall in love with each other in every way.

That's a forever that is real, lasting and achievable ... and it all starts with you.

If You Care About Me, Say It

No more empty promises and lack of action.
If you want us to work through things and I'm
the one you want, then stand up and step up.
I'm done trying to read your mind.
If we can't communicate openly and candidly
about our relationship, then I need to rethink
where my heart belongs.
I know we could have a great future, but it
takes two to put forth the effort ...
I can't keep putting my heart out there and
trying to make it work when you're just stuck in
place.
You know how I feel and what I want – I've
made that very clear.
It's time for you to do the same.
If you don't know what you want or if you're
unsure, then I'm not the one for you.
I need meaningful words backed up by honest
action ... no more empty promises or
"hopefully soons."
That's not fair to me, and I'm through trying to
guess what you want.

I love you with all my heart, but this is where two people need more than just love ... they need communication and effort.

I'm not your maybe or possibly kind of gal.

You're either all in or I'm walking away.

Not because I don't want this or because I don't care about you, but because I love myself more than to wait in a holding pattern while you "figure things out."

It shouldn't be hard to express your feelings if that's how you truly feel.

I'm worth the effort and much, much more.

I've been letting this go on for far too long, and I'm done being the one left holding my heart wondering what's going on between us.

If I'm not the one for you, just step up and tell me ... you owe me that much, at least.

I guess I've finally hit the wall where my patience has run out.

I didn't want to be this way, but it's an empty feeling wondering how your partner truly feels.

It's now or never, put up or shut up time ... Are you going to step up and make your feelings known?

If you keep waiting around expecting me to be just an option, think again.

Wait too long and in the blink of an eye, I'll be gone.

It all comes to down to this ...

Can you be the person I need or are you going to be just another broken road?

I don't need a hero, a Prince Charming or a fairy tale.

I just need real, honest and respectful.

I'm ready for forever ... are you?

I Never Knew Love Until I Was Loved By You

You were the beautiful disaster that found a
wonderful connection in me.
We were the last line to every love story and
the first verse in every love song.
Happily ever after and fairy tales didn't ever
seem to know where to find either of us until
we discovered each other.
Truth be told, we just kinda stumbled into each
other and, well, the rest is history.
Our history.
Our love story.
Not the sort of romantic adventure that features
perfect heroes and amazing times, but the real
kind with outrageous laughter, awkward
mistakes and innocent innuendos.
We didn't fall in love, we fumbled, bumbled and
stumbled our way into it.
Yet, I wouldn't change a verse in our version of
love.
I don't know who stole the light from your soul,
but I see its radiance fighting to return home.
Buried beneath the soulful expression that
guards your beautiful eyes,

193

I see the passage hidden to where I belong ...
your soul and mine, joined forever as one.
You've kept your magic stashed away for so
very long, it's amazing that it dances for me so
wonderfully now, but then, that's the way love
is supposed to be.
You shine so brightly that the stars in heaven
are jealous and love me with such passion that
sets my soul on fire.
You've set my heart ablaze and my spirit at
ease, and in your touch, I feel the excitement
of love's desire and the calm of love's
fulfillment.
I don't know what tomorrow will bring, but the
dying rays of today will find me loving you.

I'm Going To Look in the Mirror and Love the Reflection Staring Back at Me … She Is Always More Than Enough

All my life, I've fought to lift my self-esteem and build myself up.

You never really forget those times as a child or a young adult when others call you names and make fun of you ... that's something that sticks with you, always in the back of your mind.

I've worked very hard to believe in myself and exude confidence, but there are those days and times when the demons of insecurity whisper to your darkest places.

Everyone tries to tell you how to look, how to dress, how to act … all the things that really don't matter in the bigger picture of things.

But I'm guilty of chasing approval from people who pass judgement on appearance for no reason other than to try to make myself feel better ...

And truthfully, it never did.

I'm done with trying to seek the favor of those for things I don't care about.

I want to be known for the beautiful qualities I have, not how pretty I am ...

There's so much more to me than what I'm wearing or my external beauty.

Show me the way to the people who praise depth, love passion and enjoy character ... I'm walking away from all those fake people who concern themselves with unimportant details in a world obsessed with fake perfection.

I'm imperfect, I'm flawed and I'm always going to have bad days ... that's just life.

But as I look in the mirror, I know that those things don't define me, they motivate me to try harder.

My scars tell the story of where I've been, and my heart sings the melody of where I'm going.

I have times of insecurity and indecision, but we all do.

Taking a deep breath, I close my eyes and exhale slowly. Opening my eyes, I see the woman staring back at me and

I'm starting to see more than all the bad stuff I used to fixate on.

It's not easy as my eyes try to drift to my imperfections and flaws, but I know now I'm more than that. I done focusing on the things that don't matter and I'm going to begin believing in the things that do.

I'm strong because I've survived the fire and risen again.

I'm brave because I dug deeply and found the courage to start believing and loving myself in the way I always should have.

I'm loved by the people in my life who appreciate me for all of the beautiful disasters and glorious messes that make me special … and I'm now learning to put myself and my needs first … including love.

As a smile begins to curl the corners of my mouth, I start to remember the magic that has made me amazing all along.

I'm more than enough … and I always will be. This year, I'm showing myself and the world just how high I can fly.

No matter what … I got this.

Sometimes, you can love someone so much
and still, the things you say can come out all
wrong.

Not fueled by anything but love, the wrong
words can find their way into your relationship
from hidden places you didn't even know
existed.

Maybe it's self-sabotage, maybe it's fear,
maybe it's a little of both.

You don't mean to hurt them or cause them
pain, but the demons that you wrestle with
come slowly creeping back.

The insecurities and doubts, they can slowly
make their way into your subconscious ...

And the words you utter cut your love to the
bone ... and you end up in a place that you
never meant to be.

Misunderstood and reeling from pain, you wish
more than anything you could just roll back
time and take it all back ...

But you can't.

You gasp and feel as though you can't catch
your breath ...

It's then that you realize how very physical pain can be.

The silence of a hurting heart can be the most deafening of all, and there's no cure but to hope and wait.

It's a hard place to be in, not knowing where you stand or how things will turn out, only that you can't control any of it.

No matter how much you love someone, all you can do is hope for a better tomorrow and their forgiving heart.

Only time and destiny will determine where your path will take you, but if you've done all you can do, the most painful part is the waiting.

You close your eyes and hope that love is enough to make it past the mistakes and misspoken words, but you just don't know.

What's meant to be will always find a way, and that's what you tell yourself in those moments of nervous sadness.

You hope that the dawn of a new day will bring understanding and forgiveness …

But nothing is ever certain.

All you can do is wait and hope to see that name pop up on your phone as you find yourself holding your breath.

Never before would "good morning" mean so much as it does right now.

For now, in this moment, you just have to believe.

That's all you have.

You know it will be enough.

It has to be.

Love conquers all ...

At least that's what I'm hoping.

I know you think that I just gave up on us, but that's so far from the truth.
I didn't quit trying to love you, because I will always love you,
But sometimes love isn't enough … it takes effort too.
I quit trying to make it work with you because you weren't willing to do what it took for us both to be happy – not just you.
I tried to compromise, meet you halfway and do my part … but it takes two people to try, to put in the work for a relationship to be successful ... and you aren't willing to do what it takes.
So, no, I'm not choosing to give up on us,
I'm choosing myself and my own happiness over someone who says they care but then doesn't back it up with action.
I'm done believing the empty words.
I've cried so many tears and endured so many sleepless nights wanting you to just do something … anything.
I just wanted you to try.

I'm done chasing you, begging you to communicate and hope that you'll show me that I'm worth the effort.

Sadly, you've shown me how much I don't really mean to you because if I did, you would do whatever it takes to help us make it through this ... but you're not, and I don't think you ever will.

Maybe someone else would be okay with being an afterthought, but I'm not that person.

I deserve the best and I'm willing to work for it. Someday, maybe, you'll find someone that you're willing to sacrifice for, but I doubt it. That takes too much work.

So, before you spew angry words at me and blame me for quitting, take a good long look in the mirror.

I'll always love you and wish you the best, but I'm done fighting for someone who won't fight for us.

I'm going to start chasing my dreams and happiness instead ... and the thought makes me smile.

Maybe you'll realize what we had once I'm gone, but that's not my concern anymore.

I'm finally done ... I'm all out of tears.

I choose me.

Maybe I won't be happy quickly, but I'll get there.

I deserve it. I'm worth it.

I'm more than enough.

One day, someone else may see that, but I'll be fine if they don't.

I don't need anyone else to tell me how amazing I am.

I know just how awesome I am because I believe in myself in a way you never did.

My future starts with me ...

Today.

Thank you for setting me free.

Now I can finally fly again.

Strong, proud and free.

I'm done with the people who don't know what they want or wonder if I'm worth the effort.

I don't have the time for lackluster love and I'm never going to be just an option.

If you want me at my best, then step up and be your best too.

I don't play games and I don't mince words – what you see is what you get with me and that's never going to change.

Some might call me hard to please, sassy or difficult, but that's because they can't handle me.

I keep my head, my hopes and my standards high, and I'm not changing that for anyone.

I learned the hard way a long time ago to never settle for less than what I want, and I've raised my game since then.

If you want a girl, a toy or someone to kill time with, look elsewhere.

I'm not that person and I never will be.

I have a heart of gold and a passionately deep soul, and I'm worth the best anyone has to offer.

I'm done chasing the people who don't know if they want to be in my life or love me, because the ones that do … they stick around because they get me and love me just the way I am.
So, if you're going to stand around and try to figure out if you want me, then don't blink, because I'll be gone just as quickly.
I'm going to keep doing what I do, loving my life and loving my people hard, because that's who I am.
I don't have the time or patience for indecisive people who don't know what they want.
I know what I'm worth, and the people who don't won't be a part of my life.
I'm fine being on my own; I'm strong, independent and fiery ... and my people always have my back.
And that's just the beginning.
I don't believe in making wishes or having dreams that I don't chase, because that's where the magic is.
This is my life, and if you want to be part of it, stand out, step out and be real.
Rain or shine, I'm going to enjoy my life and live every day to its fullest.

It's up to you if you think you're strong enough
to be part of it.
I'm not the easiest one to love, but I'm well
worth the effort ...
Just like my life.
It may not be pretty, it may not be easy,
But at least I live it my way.

She's given so many a chance to be part of her life … but not everyone earned the chance to stay.
She'd always had an open mind and a forgiving heart, but some people came around with an agenda.
And she's done with selfish people and the takers – the ones who tried to take advantage of her, hurt her or just didn't really care about her at all.
She's washing her hands of the negative people and the toxic situations.
They've done nothing but bring her heartache and tears.
It took her a long time to realize it was okay to say goodbye to people you love –
some belong in your heart, not your life.
It was a long, painful road letting go of those people and memories ... but those were the things that made her feel badly, and she was done with being let down anymore.
Sure, she wore her emotions on her sleeve and accepted everyone at face value … but

there will always be those few who try to take advantage of anyone nice and happy.

So, she decided to close off her life and heart to those people and take control over what she wants and who she wants to share it with.

Her happiness and peace are what she values most now ... she doesn't need love, acceptance or approval to find the place where her soul is at ease.

She's surrounding herself with her people – the ones who love and accept her unconditionally, without judgment or opinion.

She's building a better tomorrow by finding the love for herself that she lost while trying to be everything for everyone else.

She learned the painful lessons of betrayal the hard way and spent many nights crying ... but it took those fires to forge her newfound spirit and courage.

She knows who she is becoming, and she's stepping above the things that try to drag her down.

Maybe she won't figure it out overnight, but she knows what she deserves and won't settle for anything less.

Rain or shine, storms or rainbows, she's
pressing forward to a better place ...
A happier place.
One in which she can always be alive and free
...
Just the way she's always wanted.
On her terms.

Yes, I will be fine ... I always am.

Even the strongest among us need a moment, so please give me that.

To catch my breath, to gather myself, to collect my thoughts. I just need to be quiet for a bit.

I know you don't understand why and think that it has something to do with you, but I promise you that it doesn't.

I love you just the same, I just need some time alone to be with myself and my thoughts.

It doesn't mean I'm mad, upset or that something is wrong with me ... it just means I need time to reflect and recharge.

I can see the struggle in your eyes. You want to help solve my challenges, but this isn't a battle you can help me fight.

I get sad, I get beaten down, I get weary sometimes.

It doesn't change who I am or how I feel about anyone, that's just my way of coping.

You're still the person I turn to, but this isn't something you do for me.

I don't expect you to understand, because truthfully, I don't totally get it myself.

It's not easy for you, I know, watching me turn inward and turn away.

But it's for the best – for me and for us.

I want our relationship to be healthy and happy, so this is what I need to keep it that way.

So, yes, I'm going to be fine. I always am.

Just hold my heart and wait for me on the other side.

I need for you to be patient as I work through things, however long that may take ... and hopefully, it won't be long.

I love you, and I'll see you after I make my peace and find my way through the stuff in my head ... the things weighing down my heart and clouding my vision.

Thank you for allowing me to do what it takes to help me get through this – I know it's hard for you to just stand by and watch.

It hurts me too, knowing your angst.

But it's what I need. It's what we need.

It's not easy, I know ... but it will be worth it.

We're worth it.

See you soon, love.

I'll be fine soon enough.

I know we've had some hard times and been through some tough days, but we're still here, fighting for each other, with love in our hearts ... believing in us no matter how hard it may get.

There are days when we can't seem to get on the same page and that's okay ...

We still find a way to make it through.

I know it hasn't always been easy, but the best things in life are worth fighting for ...

Like us.

We have a once in a lifetime love story, and I believe in us.

There are going to be stormy days and we won't always see eye to eye, but as long as we keep love in our hearts, communicate and work together, we can always find our way.

Hand in hand, heart to heart and soul to soul, we have a beautiful love that won't end.

So, as I stand in front of you, I'm just asking you to love me at my worst and celebrate me at my best, as I will do for you.

And we will keep going, keep loving and keep thriving.

No matter what happens or how hard it gets,
know that I'll never give up on us or stop loving
you.
Me, you and forever ...
That's the love story that will always be
The most wonderful one of all:
Ours.

You're Not Afraid of Love; You're Afraid That Everyone Else Is Like the Last Person Who Destroyed You

I know you're scared to trust anyone again, and I understand why, I truly do.

I realize you've been hurt so badly before, and you just don't know if you can give yourself fully to anyone ever again.

I'm here, standing before you, telling you that I don't have expectations.

I know you're worth any amount of time, and I'm willing to do whatever it takes to earn your trust and love … no matter how long that may be.

I've never met a more wonderful person with such a beautiful soul – from the moment we met, you've amazed me with everything you are.

I know your walls are high and your heart is guarded, and I don't blame you because I understand why.

I don't know exactly how you feel, but I've been in a similar place and I'm committed to sharing all of who I am with you ... My hopes, my

dreams, my fears, my vulnerabilities –
everything that makes me, well, me.

I know neither of us is perfect, but with time,
patience, communication and love, I believe we
might just find the perfect love story.

It won't be easy, but then, nothing worth having
ever is.

So, I stand before you, beholden, open and
willing to be here for you and walk with you,
hand in hand, as we grow together, day by
day.

I don't have all the answers, but I do know this
... you're worth everything to me, and I look
forward to spending my days building a future
with you.

Storms will come and days might sometimes
be hard, but you don't have to face it alone
anymore.

So, for now, let's just take it slow.

We have plenty of time ... forever is ours and
dreams don't have expirations.

Me, you and tomorrow ... for always.

I went down all the wrong roads and made all
the worst choices.

I pursued the wrong men for love, and I tried to
please people who weren't worth my efforts.

I was ignored, treated badly and cast aside like
I didn't matter.

It's a dark place when you don't think anyone
cares and everything you do goes badly.

Truth is, you stop believing in all the good stuff
and start wallowing in your misery.

I was left holding the pieces of my broken heart
so many times I didn't think love existed
anymore.

I mean, who does it really work out for?

I would shake my head and try to convince
myself that I wouldn't give another man a
chance to break my heart ... until I opened up
to another person and ended up on the same
broken road that had become all too familiar.

I'd break down and tears would cover my face.
Life would find me heartbroken.

I wondered why me?

Why couldn't I have love and happiness like all the people I would see every day?

Sometimes, it takes a friend, a moment of vision or just the realization of your situation to help you see past your darkness to know that you don't have to stay there in the unhappiness.

I couldn't keep living this way – always holding my breath waiting for the next disaster or bad news.

I had to stop treating myself like I wasn't good enough and settling for however people wanted to treat me.

I'd been broken, I'd been sad, I'd fallen … but I wasn't staying down anymore.

I wasn't going to let the fire that had consumed me every day continue to ruin my life.

It was time to stop settling, stop accepting mistreatment and start taking responsibility for my future.

It wasn't enough to just say "that's just my luck" and be okay with it any longer ... because I'm not.

I'm more than good enough, I'm worth it, and most importantly, I got this.

I look at you and see my future,
Sometimes, our love overwhelms me,
And there's nothing more I want than
To spend the rest of my days loving you.

I want to celebrate the milestones,
I want to live in the moment of our lives,
I want to soak in the beauty around us,
As our love envelopes us for always.

Many years from now,
When our faces are lined with wrinkles
From a life well lived and loved,
I want to look at you and just smile.

Happily holding your hand,
I want to think back on our memories,
Of the love and life we shared.
The times won't always be perfect ...
But it will be beautiful as long as it's with you.

I've tried to live my life the right way, fitting in the best way I know how ...
And it's exhausting.
Everyone has an opinion about who I should be, what I should do or how I should act.
But why would I listen to anyone who doesn't really know me?
They don't know where I've been, the struggles I've survived or the scars that tell my story.
I'm done trying to march to the beat of the drums of people who don't know me at all.
I don't owe anything to anyone except myself, and I've been forsaking my own needs for too long.
It's time I started living for me and seeking the things that bring me happiness.
I'm done listening to "should," "need to be" and "can't do" ...
I can do anything I set my mind to, and that's just what I'm going to do ...
I'm flipping the script and charting a new direction.

I may not know where I'm going, but wherever it is, it will be what I choose … for me, because of me.

I'm done asking for permission or approval because that's done nothing but make me unhappy ...

I deserve better than the life I've been living, and I'm going to finally start chasing my dreams and desires the way I should have a long time ago.

I'll stumble and fail, but at least I'm doing it on my own terms.

No more regrets, apologies or wishes.

This is my story, and I'm turning the page to a new chapter.

It may not always go as I plan, but at least I'm writing the way I choose.

My scars, broken parts and jagged edges make me the wonderful individual I am.

Anyone who truly loves me sees the worst and best of me and holds my hand through it all.

So, everyone can save their opinions about who I am and what I should be.

If you're willing to accept me and love me just as I am, then take my hand and let's go start living our best lives.

Rain or shine, rise or fall, I'll do it the way I should have all along.

My way.

Some stars were always meant to shine ... And that's just what I'll be …

My own kind of star.

How Many Scars Did We Justify Because We Loved the Person Holding the Knife?

Even as you were hurting me, I was making up all the reasons why it was okay.
The things you said and the way you treated me shattered my heart in countless pieces as you wreaked emotional havoc on me.
The worst part of it wasn't that you did it or that I allowed it, but that I rationalized your anger and emotional abuse.
My friends would beg me to leave and do everything they could to help free me from our toxic relationship.
But I was so lost in survival mode that I couldn't exist in any place other than where I currently was … and as bad as I was, at least it was something I knew.
Leaving it all behind … well, that scared me.
What if I wasn't strong enough, what if you came after me … those were some of the questions that made my heart race in fear.
But truthfully, sometimes you don't know how strong you truly are until being strong is the only option you have …

And on that last night, you finally pushed me so far that I didn't think I'd make it to the morning. Your rage consumed you and somehow, you tried to make me believe it was my fault.

That was the moment the clouds broke and something snapped in me.

If I didn't escape this toxicity, it would take everything from me, possibly even the breaths from my lungs.

I closed my eyes and took a deep breath and decided … no more.

I waited for the fear and uncertainty to set in … but it never did.

I believed that the thought of leaving you would cause my heart to hurt like it had so many times in the past ... but the pain never came.

I was finally numb – you had pushed me to the point where I just didn't care anymore.

I sat staring quietly at you as your eyes flashed red with the familiar ire of your dreadful rage.

Silently and deliberately, I stood up slowly and wistfully shook my head at you and your temporarily subsiding debacle ...

Tossing my house key on the table, I mustered a weak smile and uttered words I'll never forget

...

"See you around."

I knew I wouldn't, but that's all I could think of in those tense moments as I tried to maintain my composure.

I slammed the door behind me ... on you, and on my dead-end past.

And on that night that changed my life, I also opened my heart and soul to new possibilities. I still had a long hard road ahead, but finally, I was something I hadn't been in a long time.

I was free.

When I Burn, I Burn Brightest, for I Am the Phoenix

I did not fall from grace, for I was not at the top when I plunged to rock bottom.
It doesn't mean I'm capable of great things ... It just means I haven't yet found my way.
No, I had to claw my way up from the bottom. Lonely, broken and empty, I had all but fallen into complete despair.
The darkness can be comforting for a bit if you let it ... but I had to fall to my lowest to find myself midst the burning embers of what was, the forgotten dreams and broken road.
I had to face the fires of my failures to forge the courage I would need to dig my way out of the darkness.
Make no mistake – every step, every day, every battle left its mark on my soul ...
But that is where the fury of flames survived began to ignite the passions that I had long since forgotten.
Slowly, surely, I lifted myself up, remembered who I was, and my strength grew. Not out of belief, hope or courage ... but because I had no other choice.

I rose because the fires of my failed life would have consumed me whole if I had not chosen to fight back, to do more than survive ... to mend my broken wings that had once soared and would soar again.

I am born again out of the ashes of my life, with the vision to finally see my dreams again, the hope to finally believe again ... and courage to see it through.

I'm tired of being a failure, of quitting, of never becoming what I've always known I could be.

It was in those darkest moments that I realized, I had to burn in the very things that threatened to claim my soul ...

I had to do more than just face the fire, burn in my struggles and survive my life ... Instead, I became the fire, born again as a Phoenix

...And this time, I'm burning brighter than the night sky.

As I set my life and my world on fire with the fighter that is within me.

Stronger, braver and alive at long last.

What Makes You Vulnerable Also Makes You Beautiful

I was always told that tough people don't cry –
they're too strong for that.
And as I'm older now, I realize that's simply not
true.
I spent so many years trying to be the biggest,
baddest and toughest around and, truthfully, it
never made me feel any better.
It actually made me feel worse to bottle up my
emotions and repress who I truly was.
I've known for so long that I'm a sensitive and
caring person, and the world would have you
believe that those are bad qualities ...
But I don't care anymore. I'm choosing to
finally listen to my heart and be who I'm meant
to be.
I'm tired of listening to the opinions of the
people who don't care or matter.
I'm owning who I am.
I'm too strong to let the world tell me what I can
or can't be anymore.
This is my path and my choices, so I'm going
to be vulnerable because that is my truth ... my

emotions are part of who I am, and I refuse to deny them anymore.

I'm going to proudly share my vulnerabilities with the people who deserve my love.

Sure, I'll cry at all the movies and I'll get emotional for the silliest reasons, but that's who I am and always will be.

More than that, it's what makes me beautiful.

Let people think what they want about who I am, because I'm done living my life by the accord of others.

My happiness matters most and always will.

So, yes, I cry sometimes, I'm vulnerable and I can be sensitive too.

But that doesn't make me weak or immature, just the opposite.

I'm stronger for acknowledging the deepest parts of who I am and being unafraid to be real with who and what I am.

My people will always love and accept me for who I am, unconditionally.

So, to all those who think being vulnerable means you're weak, think again.

I'm strongest of all because I've embraced my true self and been brave enough to stand tall in all of my truth.

Maybe I'll never be perfect or flawless, but I'll always be true and real.
So, when you meet me and look me in the eye, know that you're seeing all of me.
No games, hiding or pretense.
I will always be able to say that I lived my life just the way I wanted to ...
As my own person, true to who I am.
I always did it ... my way.
And that means everything to me.

Goddess, Carefree, Fragile Mess: The Wonderful Chaos That Is Me

Most days, I'm a complete mess just trying to keep it together.

Running out the door, throwing on clothes as I go, being the wonderful chaos that is me.

Make no mistake, I own every bit of my beautiful disaster, from forgetting where I'm going to taking a wrong turn while talking on the phone.

To know me is to love me ... I mean, who wouldn't love a mostly happy person wearing their heart on their sleeve with a vibrant and colorful personality?

Some days, I have my act together and I walk around like I own the place.

Other days, I'm crying in the shower and sad because I can't get my hair right ...

There are greater tragedies, I know, but in those moments, it's just the end of the world it seems.

I can also live on the edge, wild and carefree ... just as easily.

That's the thing about me.

I'm an awesome combination of unusual personality and divergent attitude ...

Truthfully, I don't even know what version of me to expect most of the time.

Goddess, carefree or fragile mess.

I may be one or the other ... or perhaps a bit of all three.

Loving me is unpredictable – you never know what you're going to get when I show up – and you'll never be bored, that's for sure.

But no matter what is going on or how challenging my life may be at that moment, you can count on me to be real, authentic and heartfelt.

I don't play games and I'll be there for my people ... I love each of them with everything I have.

I'm just a person you want in your corner because I'm loyal to a fault.

And although I can be a train wreck, I make it all fun to be around.

So, if you can just hold me when I'm a mess, laugh with me when we're having fun and cry with me when life gets us down, then take my hand and let's see what mischief we can find.

I can't promise I'll always have it together –
more often than not I won't, and that's part of
my charm.
But you can count on me to always have your
back when you need me, to love hard when
there's love to be had and to do everything with
passion.
I'm a goddess some days, a wild child on
others ... even a fragile mess at times, but I'm
always right here, doing my best.
One day at a time, rise or fall,
That's all I can do,
And that's enough for me.
Why just exist when you can truly live?
Your life, you choose ...
I did.

When she met him, it was the wrong time for love … for both of them.

They had both come out of failed relationships and their fragile hearts were in pieces.

They didn't intend on meeting anyone, much less clicking with someone –anyone – it just kinda happened.

They were both scared, and she told him she couldn't risk another broken heart.

In fact, she said, she didn't even know if she really believed in love anymore.

He smiled, taking her hand in his.

"It's okay. I don't want anything from you other than your time and to just ... be."

Her brows furrowed and she studied him closely.

Never had a man come to her without expectations or demands ... simply just wanting to walk beside her for a while – however long they wanted that to be.

What a strangely nice feeling it was to be accepted just for who she was on her own terms, she thought.

She began walking and, clenching his hand a little tighter, she looked over at him, their eyes meeting serenely.

"Are you sure that's enough?"

Smiling warmly, he nodded.

They had both come to that place damaged and reeling from heartache and pain.

Sometimes, unexpected and wonderful things happen on the way to somewhere else.

They weren't looking for love, pleasure or anything in particular ...

They just wanted to walk and talk together.

In a word, they were just ... content.

In those moments, they wanted nothing, needed nothing and most importantly, expected nothing.

The only thing they were certain of is that they owned nothing but the very moment they were in ...

And for those two precious souls just trying to find their ways,

In that moment,

It was enough.

She had finally started to realize that every happily ever after wasn't the same for everyone.

She was sure that some fairy tales involved glass slippers and white picket fences, but that was never her path.

She was a strong willed, feisty and headstrong woman who didn't just accept whatever life gave her ...

No, she wasn't okay with anything less than what she knew she deserved.

She was worth the best and would spare nothing to get what she wanted.

It might mean strapping on some boots, putting in some work and fighting for it, but if that's what it took, so be it.

She was willing to pay the price for her dreams.

Her path had never been an easy one, and she thrived under the pressure of challenges.

She saw the magical stories of true love, romance and Prince Charming and shook her head.

Who did that ever happen to anyway?

She wasn't holding out for a hero; she was the heroine of her own story ...

She made her own magic and created her own opportunities, and no man would change anything about who she was.

She didn't need to be saved or fixed ... she loved her flaws and imperfections, right down to all of her jagged edges and curvy beauty.

No, she was used to fighting for what she wanted – nothing worth having ever came easy, and she knew love would be no exception.

She didn't seek the spotlight because she shined from within ... her scars told the story of her ability to overcome every fire that had tried to bring her down.

And she was still standing strong, ready for the next disaster or terrible day.

While she didn't expect life to be all rainbows and sunshine, she welcomed those beautiful parts with open arms when they showed up.

She embraced herself because she knew that she would never find her worth in another person – she would find it within herself – and then the person worthy of her love would show up when the time was right.

So, she continued to do what warriors do ...
she fought ... for her life, for her dreams, and
even for love, if necessary.

Forget the stories about glass slippers and
fairy tale endings ... her story was one of a
kind.

She was both the beauty and the beast ... and
she wouldn't have it any other way.

All my life, I had lived in fear –
Afraid of what others would think, of what bad
things could happen or fearful that someone
might not like me.
But I'm done living my life that way.
All it ever did was bring me worry, heartache
and disappointment, and I'm through letting
those negative feelings control me.
I deserve more out of my life than I've been
getting, but that's what I've been allowing ...
letting people take advantage of me, accepting
partners who treat me disrespectfully, and
allowing negativity ruin my dreams.
All of that ends here and now.
I'm taking back my life and owning my choices.
I'm done being a victim and no longer will I
allow anyone to treat me like a second-class
person.
This is my life, and I demand more.
More love, more light, more hope, more
freedom.
I'm not going to live in dread of the next
disappointment, and I refuse to listen to people
who don't have my best interests at heart.

The ones who really love me accept me as I am and will love me regardless of the choices I make.

I'm walking away from the selfish suitors, takers and all the people who try to put me down to make themselves feel better.

You know what?

I don't have it all figured out right now, other than I know that I won't accept my life the way it is anymore.

I'm going to open my mind to the possibilities and close my soul to the negativity.

I realize now that whatever happens to me is by my choice … and I choose to stand strong, no matter what life throws at me.

I know there will still be days that bring me to my knees and nights when I want to cry ... but those times are no longer going to define me.

I'm going to get stronger, better, wiser.

It won't be painless, and it won't be fast, but it's the best thing that I will ever do for myself.

I'm going to surround myself with people who believe in me, and I refuse to accept failure any longer.

I'll still stumble, and I'll still make mistakes, but that's just part of my growth.

Bad hair days, cranky moods and crying in the shower will still be part of my beautiful brokenness ... and I wouldn't have it any other way.

I've been down a hard road and survived a tough past, but I'm right where I'm supposed to be ... it's up to me to recognize the opportunity and seize my chance to evolve and rise again.

Call me broken, call me difficult, call me hard to understand ... it doesn't really matter to me.

Because what no one will ever call me again is afraid.

My time, my choice, my victory.

Rise or fall, rain or shine ...

I'll finally be able say I did it my way.

I had been down for so long I had almost become comfortable in the misery.

That's the thing about being defeated – it saps your will to pick yourself up and clouds your vision to see beyond your situation.

I didn't have any answers and didn't know what the next day would bring ...

Only that I had two choices:

Either get busy living or get busy dying.

I'd had enough of the darkness, dreading my life and feeling sorry for myself.

Something had to change, and I realized that it had to be me.

I just had to make up my mind to stop dwelling and start fighting back.

I knew it would be the fight of my life, but I also knew that I had what it took to rise again.

I refused to accept that my life was over and that I was powerless to change it all.

Maybe it wouldn't be fast, easy or painless, but I could do it.

I would be fine ... somehow, someday soon ...

I'd figure it out and start seeing a new path.

241

More than that, I'd dig and claw until I found my joy again ... joy in the moments of my life, in my heart and most importantly, in my soul.

I'd stopped believing in myself for so long that I knew what lie ahead was the battle of my life.

I took a deep breath, closed my eyes and hit play on my music ...every day, my soul slowly started to come to life a little more, a little stronger.

I was tired of living a day away from disaster and a heartbreak away from giving up.

Maybe I don't have wings right now, but I do have claws ... and I'm going to dig myself out of this hole, take back my life, find my voice and start a new chapter.

I'm saying goodbye to all the ones who turned their backs on me and said I'd never make it ... turns out you didn't know me at all.

So, as you shake your head in disbelief as I rise up from the ashes, know that you were always going to be wrong about me.

I'm a warrior phoenix, and nothing can stop me once my mind is made up.

I'm not meant to survive, manage or get by.
Not even close.

I'm meant for so much more than that.

My life, my way, my time.

I'm saying goodbye to the person I used to be ... because I'm never going back there again.

I'm reborn of struggle and strife, fire and failure ... and I'm growing stronger by the day.

It's a new day and a new life ...

The brightest diamonds are forged under pressure ... and that's just what I'm going to do, darlin' ...

Shine on ...

Like the beautiful diamond I was always meant to be.

From the very first moment we connected, we just knew.

We didn't need time, conversation or even eye contact to tell us what we both instantly realized about us.

There was something very different about the way our souls met, unlike anything we'd ever known.

It left us speechless with wonder, amazement and gratitude.

I spent so long trying to make the wrong ones fit into the right places that I almost stopped trying ... then one comes along that fits so perfectly in all the ways you'd always dreamed but never believed possible.

I became awestruck with the depth and intensity of our connection, the beauty of our attraction, and the wonder of it all ...

How we found each other in a sea of souls and were so perfectly meant for each other beyond compare.

There's no way I could have ever foreseen you and how you just understood me from the beginning ...

On all levels in all the ways.

Mind, body, spirit, heart and soul.

As I tried to find the words to tell you how much you meant to me, how amazing I thought you were and how thankful I was to find you ... nothing could begin to describe my feelings for you.

You loved my imperfections and embraced all my flaws.

You adored my deepest vulnerabilities.

No one had ever accepted and loved me just as I was, until you.

In fact, you looked deeply into my soul and whispered so softly to me ...

"Don't ever change."

So, forgive me if the only words that I can truly find to express all the things you are to me don't speak my heart enough, but they'll have to do, for now.

And I'll spend the rest of our life together showing you just how very special you are to me.

Soul-to-soul and heart-to-heart ...

Your hand in mine, our hearts beating as one, forever and always ...

'Til death us part ... and even longer if we can.

I shall and always will adore you ...
I love you.

It Wasn't That She Was Changing, It Was That She Was Finally Becoming Herself

All around her people remarked about how very different she had become.

Gone was the meek and soft-spoken girl, and in her place stood a strong, defiant woman.

Everyone was astounded at how much she'd changed, saying she wasn't the same person she used to be.

She'd smile as she heard the whispers about her from the people who didn't know what to make of her now.

She'd always known that people feared change and the things they didn't understand ...

And no one seemed to get why she chose to evolve like she had.

They'd scoff and say she was weak and trying to be like everyone else.

They'd rationalize and come up with countless reasons why she wasn't the same woman she used to be ...

But what none of them understood was that she hadn't chosen to change, like they called it

...

Her evolution was something completely different ... more beautiful, more original. Sure, she was a totally different person to everyone she once knew ... but not for the reasons they thought.

She had done what so many of them had thought was impossible:

She was finally becoming the person that she was meant to be all along.

She'd fought, grown and evolved into a stronger, wiser and happier woman whose confidence shined onto everyone around her.

She'd fallen, she'd struggled, and she'd failed along the way ...

But that wasn't how her story was ever going to end.

No, those struggles didn't define her, they forged her new path to greater heights and a stronger heart.

She didn't need anyone's approval or acceptance of the road she traveled, because she knew that she was exactly where she was meant to be.

It was her life to live and her dreams to chase.

She put away the claws that helped her climb
out of the failures and found what she'd
searched her whole life for:
Her wings.
It was her time to become everything she'd
ever wanted.
She rose up and chose to fly high, breathe free
and always seek the sunlight ...
That's who she was and where she was
headed ... for bigger, better things.
She smiled.
She had finally come home,
And everything was possible,
Because she believed –
In herself, her strength and her ability to do
anything she set out to accomplish.
No, she was more than just different or original
...
She was one of a kind.

Love Is the Person You Miss When Everyone Else Is Around You

I could be in a room full of people,
with good times and happy moments,
Music, fun and laughter filling the air,
And I'd still miss you by my side.

No matter where life takes me,
Or the joy it brings to my heart,
Everything just feels incomplete,
Until I can share it all with you.

Surrounded by my family and friends,
Celebrating, enjoying the moment …
Unless you are by my side, holding my hand,
It just doesn't feel right.

I can't explain our deep connection,
But I can feel you across a room or miles
away,
Something deeper than I've ever known,
Ties my heart and soul beautifully to yours.

Once, I swore never to need another,
To stand strong on my own, defiant and proud,
To never be beholden to my heart and feelings,
Until you came into my life and changed it all.

Now, in the blink of an eye from worlds apart,
You have become my everything,
My best friend, my lover, my soulmate, my
heart,
And the one thing I could never
Live without is you, ever again.

She hasn't walked the easiest path, but she's not one to give up easily.

She's an independent woman who fights for what she wants and doesn't settle for less than she deserves.

She's gone down the broken roads and battled the sleepless nights of heartache and tears ... And come out the other side stronger.

If you want to know who she is, look past her eyes and forget about how she looks ... those things don't define her and never will.

She's not just a woman, she's a warrior who's forged her heart from the fires of survival.

She's built walls around her heart to protect herself from the ones who will never be worth her energy or attention.

But more than that, she doesn't need anyone to make her happy, complete her or save her.

She proved to herself long ago that she's got what it takes to keep going, be happy and chase her dreams.

Sure, the road gets lonely at times, but she'll never sacrifice who she is or what she wants for just anyone's company.

She's stronger and better than that because she's perfectly fine being alone ... she's lived solo much of her life – she knows it's better to be alone than to be stuck in a dead-end relationship, because she's done both.

She knows the games some men play and sees past the temporary pleasures that so many pursue.

She needs more than that.

She craves so much more than one night can ever bring her.

She's quite content to enjoy her own company, love herself and grow through her life.

There are those moments, though, when something pulls at her heart and she wishes she had her person to share the night and days with, the victories and failures ...

Just someone she could make memories with ... but dreams aren't weaknesses. Sometimes knowing what you want is the first step on the path to finding it.

And she'll never be okay with letting just anyone be that person.

She knows who she is and what she wants …
and understands her worth.
Whoever her person is will get that about her
and much more.
So, until love comes knocking, she'll keep
living, loving and dreaming with all her heart.
Her story, her way.
Nothing else will ever do for a one-of-a-kind
woman like her.

I'm lying in bed, so tired ... but yet, I can't
sleep.
My mind refuses to relax and there's no way to
stop my thoughts, no matter how exhausted
my body may be.
More than that, my soul is weary.
Tired of all the things that have been dragging
me down lately.
Tired of fighting for survival, trying to find a way
to make it every day ...
I don't even have a moment's peace
sometimes.
There is always ... something.
Something that needs my attention, that breaks
my heart a little, that drains my energy, that
hurts my feelings.
As I lie here in the dark, there's no words for
what I'm feeling.
The emotions of a hard road defy description
... only that I'm worn out.
You stop trying to be happy after a while and
just try to survive.

I don't know what tomorrow may bring, and there's always this foreboding sense that I'm just waiting for the next disaster to come my way.

It's terrible, really, to feel captive to your own life ...

Having no control over anything is a helpless feeling.

I don't have any answers ... nor even the questions to ask.

All I know is I need rest –

For my body, my heart ... my soul.

I close my eyes and try to think back to a simpler, happier time when my dreams were new and life was brimming with possibility.

Where did I lose my hope along the way?

I exhaled loudly.

I had hit the wall ... I knew I couldn't go on like this ...

Not anymore.

No longer will I allow my life to control me ...

No longer will I just survive.

I'm better than that.

I don't know how, but I'm taking my life back.

I'll figure it out like I've always done before.

I'm done being a survivor, so weary that even my soul cries for rest.

I'm coming back a warrior.

It's going to be hard, but nothing worth having comes easy ...

And my life is worth it.

My happiness is worth it.

As sleep slowly comes, I drift off to a single thought:

I'm worth it ... and I can do it.

Tomorrow, I'm starting a new chapter.

I'm finding my way back to myself, to my happiness.

No more excuses, no more pity parties.

I'd forgotten that I had claws all along ...

So, I'm finally fighting my way out of this darkness ...

Until I can see is the light ...

Starting with tomorrow –

Starting with me.

Here's to my friends – the ones who are always there for me.

Sometimes, they show up before I even realize that I need them.

They're always there when I reach out to them, without question or judgement.

They've always loved me when I needed it most and even sometimes when I deserved it least.

They stand beside me through the heartbreaks and failures, holding me together when I can't do it myself.

They laugh with me about life's absurdities and cry with me through the tragedies.

They've got my back when I don't even ask for it. No matter where the chips may fall or what will happen, I know that they always have my back like I have theirs … and I wouldn't have it any other way.

Truthfully, I don't know where I'd be without my tribe – my BFFs, my besties, my ride-or-dies, my soul sisters.

They make it all worthwhile.

They always pick up my calls and never make me feel bad for loving the wrong guy.

Most of all, no matter how long it's been or where they are, we pick up right where we left off ... that's just who we will always be.

So, thank you to my people who have loved me through it all. I don't know how I would've made it without you.

You're more than amazing or beautiful to me, you're everything.

Thank you for being so dear and close to my heart. I love you for being just who you are ... my friends.

There's no place I'd rather be than in your hearts. It's a wonderful feeling having you in my life.

You're the family I choose ... each and every day.

You're loved more than you will ever know.

Thank you for everything you are, everything you do and everything you mean to me ... But most of all, thank you ... Just for being you.

Because at the End of the Day, You're the Person I Want To Come Home To

You're my person ...
The one I want to share everything with.
My hopes, my dreams, my fears, my victories.
I want to come home at the end of my days,
wrap up in your arms and just breathe in the
comfort of your love.
I want to sit across from you and just talk about
my days and all the things in them.
My frustrations, my happiness, my sadness
and my successes.
Whenever something happens in my life –
good or bad – you're the one I can't wait to
share it with.
Truthfully, I can't imagine life without you
holding my hand and protecting my heart.
You're the one who excites me and calms me
at the same time ...
My joy and my peace ...
You put my soul at ease when nothing else
can.
I don't know what tomorrow may bring or what
challenges life will throw at us, but so long as
you're by my side,

There's nothing we can't make it through,
Together.
Me and you, forever and always.
That's what I think about when I fall asleep
each night and my first thought upon rising
every morning.
In your arms, by your side and in your heart ...
There's no place else I'd rather be,
For the rest of my life.

Sometimes the Healing Hurts Worse Than the Wound

She'd cried herself to sleep so many nights,
trying to find a way to mend her broken heart.
What had begun not so long ago as a beautiful
love affair had slowly decayed into something
different … something unhealthy.
She couldn't tell you how she ended up in that
place, filled with angst and darkness, only that
the weight of the emotions felt oppressive.
It was worst when night fell and she was alone
with her thoughts … her feelings.
She couldn't sleep, barely ate and most of all,
couldn't stop her mind from thinking … about
everything.
Everything that had happened, where she'd
been or wondering how to make things better.
She had so many questions … and so few
answers.
The pain of the recent past burned into her
relentlessly, the words he had said that had
torn her apart.
She tried to understand why he could be that
way to her,
Someone he claimed to love dearly …

That's when the reality hit her like a load of stones.

He didn't love her as much as he loved himself and probably never would.

A solitary tear rolled down her cheek as the pain permeated her heart, and she fought to not be overwhelmed with the sudden rush of emotions.

As much as her heart screamed to stay and fight, her mind whispered what she already knew: she had to leave.

Her soul was weary from trying to save a relationship that had fallen apart some time ago.

It takes two people, she knew, to communicate and work through the problems that arise ...

And he wasn't willing to put in the effort.

She tried to tell herself that it wasn't because he didn't care, but for other reasons that she couldn't explain ...

Truthfully, she didn't have to.

The road ahead would be harder than where she'd been, but she didn't have a choice and she knew it would be worth it.

It was either move on or lose herself in the misery of a failed love ...

And she couldn't do that to herself anymore. She was better than that and deserved to be happy.

With a heavy heart, she knew she would never find happiness with him the way she wanted.

It was time.

She had to break free and find her wings again.

For so long, she had forgotten who she was and even how to fly high like she used to do.

She wiped away the tears and ran her hands through her hair, taking a deep breath and closing her eyes.

It was time to start a new chapter.

It would hurt, she knew. She'd miss him more than she wanted ... but she missed herself most of all.

Sometimes, the healing hurts worse than the wound ...

But it was a road she had to take if she ever wanted to be happy again.

Her time, her story.

The next chapter, she'd finally return home to herself ...

And it was long overdue.

Yes,
You are strong enough to survive this.
I know it seems like your world is over and
maybe you can't find the light right now, but
hang in there.
I know your soul is weary and you feel like you
can't keep going, but don't stop.
Your happiness may seem so far away, but it's
not as far as you might think.
Yes, the nights can be long, and you don't
have any answers,
But you don't have to.
Breathe.
Take a moment and remember what all you've
survived before now.
You've been through the fire and always found
your way … your courage has been forged in
the fires that tried to take you down.
Remember that – you're a warrior who will
continue to rise again.
It's time to find your magic and listen to your
heart.
It knows the way, but you've gotten so weary
that you've lost sight of the path.

If you've lost faith in yourself and your strength is waning, know that you're not alone.

You're loved, you're enough, and I believe in you.

It's always darkest before the dawn, and this is your time to start again.

Every end is a new beginning, and your next chapter will be magical ...

You just have to start believing in yourself like I believe in you.

Like all the people in your life do.

I know you're reading this and wondering how you'll make it through, but I'm telling you ...

You've got this.

You are meant for more than to simply fizzle out like a dampened flicker of light.

You're a wildfire capable of setting your soul and life on fire again.

Take my hand and let's start climbing out of the darkness, day by day.

I know you've been looking for a sign, something to believe in ...

Well, this is it.

Today is your wake-up call, and this is where you start again – you're strong enough and you're worth it.

It won't be easy, and it won't be fast, but it will change your life if you're ready.
These words were meant for you.
Are you ready to start again?
Believe, Darlin' … in you, your destiny and most of all, in that you are meant for more.
Beginning today … get up, step up and start remembering the magic and dreams you lost along the way.
Anything's possible if you just believe …
And I believe in you.

I gave you everything I had … heart, mind, body and soul.

It still wasn't good enough.

You made me feel horrible about myself in so many ways every day for reasons that didn't even matter.

The worst part was that you justified every mean thing you did and all the cruel words that you spewed at me …

Saying you were just trying to help me get better.

Get better at feeling worse about myself?

We fought so many times because you had to have the last word, you were always right … or so you thought.

I don't know when we stopped loving and started fighting for our survival as a couple, but it doesn't matter anymore.

I'm sure you'd have an answer and would blame it on me if you could …

But I'm not asking you, because you've pushed me so far that I'm not crying anymore.

I'm just numb now.

Numb to your words, your promises and your apologies.

I have nothing left to give. I've spent everything I had trying to save a relationship that I'm not even sure you care about ...

Or at least that you don't care about as much as you do yourself.

There're so many things that I'll never understand ... but I don't have to.

I've run out of words, feelings and the energy to try to care about you anymore.

It's time now to put myself first, something I haven't done in a long time ... that stops now.

Don't get me wrong, I hope the best for you, sincerely.

Just not as a part of my life.

I'm hard enough on myself without you adding to the onslaught.

So, as you're wondering why I'm not calling you back and not fighting with you on text anymore, the reason is very simple ... and powerful.

I'm done.

No more chances or trying to work things out.

I'm walking away, lifting my head up and trying to find the light again.

I know I've got a hard road ahead of me and I'll probably miss you a lot, but truthfully, I miss me more.

I miss the old me, loving, beautiful and strong ... the woman who could do anything and was always finding the happiness in her life.

I don't blame you for anything – I take responsibility for every time I allowed you to treat me badly and all the ways that I didn't stand up for myself.

That's also why I'm taking responsibility for my life back and walking away.

I'm owning my choices and my happiness,

Finally, after way too long allowing myself to feel like a victim,

Because I'm not.

I'm closing this chapter of my life and starting anew.

I don't know where I'm going or how I'll get there, but as I say goodbye to a past filled with anguish, I'm starting to finally feel the sunlight again.

Now, it's my time to get my shine back.

It's my time again ...

To rise again, to fly high and most of all,

To just be happy.

Not Everyone You Lose Is a Loss

I saw your face pop up on my phone, and a flood of memories washed over me.

It seems like a lifetime ago that our love was new, when possibilities were endless, and I thought we would be forever.

Truthfully, I don't even know anymore why we didn't work out … only that I'm happier now than I've ever been.

While I can't remember why we fell apart, I'll never forget the lessons I learned from the heartache of our breakup.

I was forced to stand on my own again and find the courage to create my own path.

It's scary being alone when you haven't been solo in so long, but I discovered it gets a little easier every day as your strength grows.

Sure, I had days when I was still sad and missing us, but I realized that I missed being a part of a couple … not necessarily you.

There was a reason why we didn't make it, and I needed to find myself again after having lost myself in you for so long.

It hurt for so long until, one day … it just didn't.

Now, that all seems like another life and my days are so different … so much happier.

I wish you all the best in whatever life path you choose, and I hope all of your dreams come true … just not with me.

So, as I see your name pop up, I don't have any desire to answer. I'm going to leave the past just where it is.

It doesn't have any place in my life and, if I answered your call, it might just make me hurt again.

As I decline your call, I sigh in relief and realize that I'm doing just what I need to be doing … leaving the past where it's meant to stay so I can keep building a happy future today.

This is my life, and these are my choices.

I didn't lose you … I found myself.

It was the best discovery I could have ever made.

Your Love Is a Beacon of Hope

When I was at my very lowest,
Trapped inside the places in my head
Dwelling in the darkness that bound me,
You found me there and led me back.

For so long, I had lingered in the places
That I hated about myself,
Never knowing why I felt the way I did,
Lacking the strength to fight my way out.

Your love was a beacon of hope
That I never expected nor knew existed,
You showed up when I needed you most,
And loved me without condition.

You embraced the darkest parts of me
Without hesitation or fail,
Dancing with my demons as you smiled,
Singing to my angels with your love.

So, as I bury my face into your embrace,
I know what it means to find someone
Who will always feel like home,
Because that is just what I found in you,
Now and for always.

She's the one who no one knew how to handle, smashing the eggshells that everyone else tiptoed on.

She tore through labels and defied definitions – she would never be limited by what anyone else thought of her … ever.

She loved as she lived – fiercely, passionately and without apology.

She wasn't just a beauty or a beast, she was both in one package … a fascinating force of nature.

Men craved her but couldn't withstand her, and other women admired her never say die attitude and individuality.

Regardless of how you felt about her, you'd never forget the day this whirlwind of a woman blew into your life.

She knew what she wanted, and she accepted nothing less than the very best of whatever life had to offer.

Her soul was deep and passionate.

Her heart was brave and loyal.

Her mind was strong and agile.

Her love was … unforgettable.

Whether friend, partner or even foe, she left her mark wherever she traveled.

She didn't care about being beautiful, accepted or loved ...

She trusted the universe to bring what she needed into her life and she'd do the rest from there.

Forget the fairy tales, romances and happily ever afters, she craved something deeper and more real than any of those fantasies.

Of course, she pursued her happiness where the opportunity lie; she wasn't content to sit back and just let life happen.

She owned her voice and her life, making no excuses and accepting no failures to be permanent.

Her passions burned brighter than her fears, and her eyes glowed with the ferocity of a woman in charge of her destiny.

She'd never water down who she was to please anyone else, and her spirit was unmistakable.

The world would never really know what to make of this warrior woman, and it didn't have to.

There's no force anywhere greater than the will of a woman determined to rise, and that's just who she was.

A woman, born of struggle's fire with a heart forged in the flames of failures overcome.

She'd never forget where she'd been or what she was meant to be.

Most of all, you'd never forget this fiery woman.

She was the one who'd been through hell, but kept going ...

And she never stopped smiling the whole time.

In a World Full of Wrongs, You Choose To Always See What Is Right

All my life, people were trying to make me conform to their standards of what was right and how I should be.
They tell you to be yourself and then judge you if they don't approve of your choices.
For so long, that's just how I thought everything and everyone would always be ... Until I met you.
You didn't criticize my flaws; you celebrated my imperfections.
You saw the person that I stowed behind placid eyes and slowly began to win my trust ... And eventually, my heart and soul.
You didn't push, force or overwhelm –
You just let me be myself and loved me for everything I was in a way that I'd never known.
In an instant, you changed the story of my life with a chapter I couldn't have seen coming.
I thought the world was full of the same people doing the same things thinking the same way
...
You proved me wrong, and I've never been happier to be incorrect in my life.

It's so much more than just love, too.

You accept me unconditionally – all my jagged edges and broken pieces. Without question or hesitation, you hug them tightly and make me realize that everything will be okay.

You've shown me that love isn't a word, it's a powerful feeling that escapes definition and changed my world, my heart and my mindset.

You love me in such a way that it empowers me to love myself, my life and my future with relentless optimism.

I've come to learn that the darkness will find every one of us at times, and what matters is how we persevere.

Taking your hand, I know that we will always make our way through it.

The good times and the bad, big things and little … they all exist in brighter colors because of the love you've showered me with.

You're patient with my disastrous days, understanding through my emotional moods and most of all, you're just there for me, whenever I need you to be.

The moment you walked into my life, I knew why it had never worked out with anyone else.

Thank you for being you.

There's no place I would rather be than right
beside you,
For the rest of our lives.

You Cannot Love Yourself and Someone Who Hurts You Simultaneously. Please Choose You

She had broken down so many times, she didn't know if her heart could take much more. Her friends had all told her to get out, but she couldn't see clearly, looking from the inside out.

She had given the relationship everything she had, and it had been a series of ugly fights and lies that tore her apart just a little more every time.

She cried herself to sleep countless nights and nursed a drink way too often as a way to numb the pain.

She'd been fighting for survival for so long, she had forgotten how to be happy ... or even what she was even fighting for.

Truthfully, she didn't even know why they were together anymore ...

Maybe it was convenience and being comfortable ... or perhaps she was afraid of being alone.

But as she raised her head to look in the mirror, one look at her own tear-stained face shook her to the core.

Where once had stood a bright beautiful girl determined to change the world now stood a tired and haggard woman who was just weary. Tired of the fights, the disasters ... of a person who hurt her even as he was telling her he loved her.

She shook her head slowly.

No more.

She wasn't this person she saw in the mirror – that wouldn't be her legacy.

No longer would she try to fix a man who was determined to break her a little more every day. It wouldn't be easy, it wouldn't be fast, but she had to get out while she had her soul intact.

She knew he would threaten her as he always did, the angry rage that personified him perfectly ... but it didn't matter anymore.

She wasn't scared.

She was utterly done.

She had to find herself again, and she couldn't do that being with him.

She deserved so much more.

She picked up her phone and dialed a number.

Her closest friend answered quickly, expecting yet another late-night distress call.

Her voice cracked as she mustered up her courage ...

"Can I come stay with you? I'm getting out ... finally."

The warmth in her friend's voice told her she was making the right choice.

She was taking her life back.

The tear that rolled down her cheek wouldn't be the last one she would shed ... but it would be the last one because of him.

She had finally realized what she had been unable to see for so long –

She couldn't love herself and love someone who hurt her at the same time.

That wasn't love, it was something twisted that had been eating away at her for all this time.

Now, it was time for her to take back her life and rise again.

It wouldn't be easy, but she knew the road ahead would end up much better than the one she'd been down.

It was her time ... to live free and find the joy in her life again.

...

Finally time to regain her wings and fly free.
She thought back to that bright-eyed girl she
once was and smiled.

"I'm coming home, darling."

For as long as she could remember, she was different ... Not in a way that people found odd, just the opposite, in fact.

People were drawn to her bubbly personality and bright smile, her warm and inviting demeanor.

But there was also something unique about her that most couldn't put their finger on – intangible and elusive, they couldn't help but be drawn to her deep and soulful eyes.

She sparkled as she spoke, and she wove magic with words ... to the point where you'd find yourself breathless.

She was one of the rare ones – a dreamer who believed she could do anything.

She glided when she walked and enchanted when she smiled.

Men, women and children all gravitated towards her effervescent charm.

She believed what the others couldn't – that she could change the world just by being herself.

She didn't know how or when, only she that
she would.
Wide-eyed and wonderful, she had a way
about her that defied description ...
But then, that's true about most beautiful things
– you can't really describe them no matter how
hard you try.
She loved with all of her heart and dreamed
with all of her soul, truly believing that anything
was possible.
She would often smile and remind you that
miracles happen every day, all around us ...
sometimes, all it takes is for you to believe.
So, as I watched her share her heart and
brighten the world for so many she touched, I
couldn't help but sigh.
Sometimes, the most beautiful miracles are the
little ones that happen right in front of us, every
day.
Change a heart, open some eyes, heal a soul.
She knew that which many of us forget as we
grow older – some of life's most wonderful
magic is within us all along, just waiting for us
to remember ...
That anything is possible when you believe.

I was a person who stopped believing in happily ever after. My heart had been shattered countless times, and I'd cried myself to sleep so many nights, how could I ever believe that true love would ever find me?

I was so fixated on all the closed doors that I couldn't see the open chances just waiting to be found.

So, I did what everyone does – I built high walls around my heart, I guarded my emotions and started being pessimistic.

But it wasn't until I started truly working on myself that anything changed ... and that's when everything shifted.

My love for myself was the one thing I had always neglected before ... but not anymore.

Before, I would see love in all the wrong partners. Dead ends, heartbreakers and fixer uppers just seemed to be attracted to me without fail.

Looking for love meant finding all the wrong answers.

When I stopped looking outside and started loving myself ... That's when you showed up.

I didn't want to trust you or believe you –
I especially didn't want to give you a chance.
But your patience and ability to see me for who
I truly was slowly melted the jaded ice around
my heart.
Months ago, I couldn't have even dreamed you
... now, I can't see my life without you in it.
It wasn't the crazy and reckless love affair of
times past – it was so much more and different
in all the right ways.
Respectful, soulful and patient love that has
grown steadily every single day ... That is what
you have given me.
I once had a heart that swore true love wasn't
real – you made me believe when I had all but
given up hope.
When I look at you now, with love in my eyes
and passion in my soul, I'm thankful for all the
broken roads, shattered dreams and sleepless
nights that led me straight to you.

She's done looking back, questioning herself
and dwelling on her mistakes.
She's rising like the dawn of a new day,
brighter, stronger and more powerful than
she's ever been.
All her life, she's battled, struggled and fought
for everything's she's ever wanted.
She didn't get the big breaks or help to climb
the mountains that she faced.
She's more than a survivor, she's a warrior
queen with a fiery spirit and a strong heart.
No longer will she allow others to take
advantage of her, and she's turning the page
on a new chapter ... today.
No more excuses, no more apologies.
This day has been a long time coming ...
The day she started fighting for her dreams
and stopped settling for less than she deserves
– in love, in life and in all the things that matter.
She's casting aside the pain of her often-
broken heart, and she's using that anguish as
fuel for her to rise stronger from the ashes.
Sure, she's afraid and doesn't have all the
answers, but she knows she doesn't have to.

She just has to get up, keep going and take each day and each step one at a time.

Courage isn't the absence of fear, but the knowledge that some things are more important ... her happiness, her life, her self-worth, her friends.

Those are worth any price, and she's going to battle for what she believes in.

She's been beaten down, dragged through failure and broken more times than she can remember ...

But those challenges never defined her ... they forged her will in the fires that tried to consume her.

The flames made her the warrior she is.

Her time is now and she's rising.

She's taking back her life, and her voice will be heard with resounding conviction.

This day is long overdue and she's seizing it with both hands.

She's standing in front of the storms that sought to bring her to her knees.

She's stared adversity, disaster and failure in the eyes before ...

But she's not wavering anymore.

She's strong, she believes, and she knows she will continue to ascend.

She has but a single thought as she charges forth into the struggles and fires that once almost ruined her ... that almost convinced her that she couldn't withstand the fury of life: "Today, I become the storm ..."